STERLING BIOGRAPHIES

Davy Crockett

Frontier Legend

George E. Stanley

STERLING

New York / London
www.sterlingpublishing.com/kids

To Gwen—my inspiration!

STERLING and the distinctive Sterling logo are registered trademarks of
Sterling Publishing Co., Inc.

Library of Congress Cataloging-in-Publication Data

Stanley, George Edward.
  Davy Crockett : frontier legend / by George Edward Stanley.
    p. cm. — (Sterling biographies)
  Includes bibliographical references and index.
  ISBN-13: 978-1-4027-5499-9
  ISBN-10: 1-4027-5499-X
  1. Crockett, Davy, 1786-1836—Juvenile literature. 2. Pioneers—Tennessee—Biography—
Juvenile literature. 3. Frontier and pioneer life—Tennessee—Juvenile literature. 4. Tennessee—
Biography—Juvenile literature. 5. Legislators—United States—Biography—Juvenile literature.
6. United States. Congress. House—Biography—Juvenile literature. 7. Alamo (San Antonio,
Tex.)—Siege, 1836—Juvenile literature. I. Title.

F436.C95S73 2008
976.8'04092—dc22
[B]

                                                                        2007048196

10 9 8 7 6 5 4 3 2 1

Published by Sterling Publishing Co., Inc.
387 Park Avenue South, New York, NY 10016
© 2008 by George E. Stanley
Distributed in Canada by Sterling Publishing
c/o Canadian Manda Group, 165 Dufferin Street
Toronto, Ontario, Canada M6K 3H6
Distributed in the United Kingdom by GMC Distribution Services
Castle Place, 166 High Street, Lewes, East Sussex, England BN7 1XU
Distributed in Australia by Capricorn Link (Australia) Pty. Ltd.
P.O. Box 704, Windsor, NSW 2756, Australia

Printed in China
All rights reserved

Sterling ISBN 978-1-4027-6057-0 (hardcover)
Sterling ISBN 978-1-4027-5499-9 (paperback)

For information about custom editions, special sales, premium and
corporate purchases, please contact Sterling Special Sales
Department at 800-805-5489 or specialsales@sterlingpublishing.com.

Designed by Audrey Hawkins for SimonSays Design!
Image research by Larry Schwartz

Contents

Events in the Life of Davy Crockett

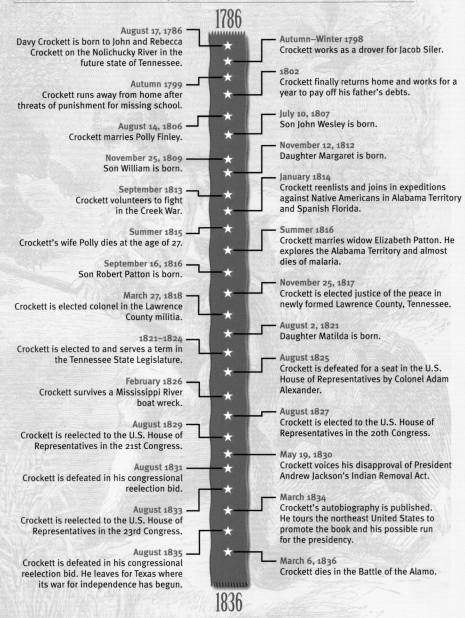

1786

August 17, 1786
Davy Crockett is born to John and Rebecca Crockett on the Nolichucky River in the future state of Tennessee.

Autumn–Winter 1798
Crockett works as a drover for Jacob Siler.

Autumn 1799
Crockett runs away from home after threats of punishment for missing school.

1802
Crockett finally returns home and works for a year to pay off his father's debts.

August 14, 1806
Crockett marries Polly Finley.

July 10, 1807
Son John Wesley is born.

November 25, 1809
Son William is born.

November 12, 1812
Daughter Margaret is born.

September 1813
Crockett volunteers to fight in the Creek War.

January 1814
Crockett reenlists and joins in expeditions against Native Americans in Alabama Territory and Spanish Florida.

Summer 1815
Crockett's wife Polly dies at the age of 27.

Summer 1816
Crockett marries widow Elizabeth Patton. He explores the Alabama Territory and almost dies of malaria.

September 16, 1816
Son Robert Patton is born.

November 25, 1817
Crockett is elected justice of the peace in newly formed Lawrence County, Tennessee.

March 27, 1818
Crockett is elected colonel in the Lawrence County militia.

August 2, 1821
Daughter Matilda is born.

1821–1824
Crockett is elected to and serves a term in the Tennessee State Legislature.

August 1825
Crockett is defeated for a seat in the U.S. House of Representatives by Colonel Adam Alexander.

February 1826
Crockett survives a Mississippi River boat wreck.

August 1827
Crockett is elected to the U.S. House of Representatives in the 20th Congress.

August 1829
Crockett is reelected to the U.S. House of Representatives in the 21st Congress.

May 19, 1830
Crockett voices his disapproval of President Andrew Jackson's Indian Removal Act.

August 1831
Crockett is defeated in his congressional reelection bid.

March 1834
Crockett's autobiography is published. He tours the northeast United States to promote the book and his possible run for the presidency.

August 1833
Crockett is reelected to the U.S. House of Representatives in the 23rd Congress.

August 1835
Crockett is defeated in his congressional reelection bid. He leaves for Texas where its war for independence has begun.

March 6, 1836
Crockett dies in the Battle of the Alamo.

1836

The Legend of Davy Crockett

Burn Crockett with the other rebels.

—*General Antonio López de Santa Anna, March 6, 1836*

In the darkness, Davy Crockett could hear the deafening cries, warning them that the Mexican army was headed their way. He couldn't see who was shouting and didn't recognize the voice. He was in San Antonio, at the Alamo, and there were only a handful of them left. Travis was dead. Bowie was dead. Most of his fellow Tennesseans were dead, too, but he knew he had a mission to finish. He readied himself as the door was flung open, and he and the other men rushed out.

They saw hundreds of Mexican soldiers running toward them. He raised his rifle and started firing. Several of the Mexicans fell, but others filled in their ranks. Suddenly, the man beside Crockett fell. He stopped to help him, but it was too late—the man was dead.

When Crockett looked up, a Mexican soldier was standing above him, grinning. His sword was aimed right at Crockett's heart.

It is easy to believe that Davy Crockett simply grinned back at his attacker. There were many times when his life had hung by a thread—especially when he was exploring the untamed western frontier or confronting ferocious black bears face-to-face. For his entire life, he had also fought against the **tyranny** of ruthless men—and he knew that one day he would meet a savage death.

CHAPTER 1

Child of the Frontier

There must therefore be something in me, or about me, that attracts attention, which is even mysterious to myself.

Davy Crockett was born on August 17, 1786, in a cabin on the banks of the Nolichucky River in Greene County, North Carolina. Although his parents, John and Rebecca, already had four sons, and a fifth son meant another mouth to feed, they welcomed him, because a son to help with the work was always an asset on the frontier. Davy was named after his grandfather Crockett, who, along with his grandmother, had been killed by Creek warriors eight years earlier during a surprise attack on their nearby farm.

When Davy was born, the state of North Carolina stretched from the Atlantic Ocean to the Mississippi River. Greene County would one day be in the new state of Tennessee. In fact, by the time of Davy's birth, Americans

In 1786, the year Davy Crockett was born, the United States was about one-third the size it is today, and the state of North Carolina stretched all the way from the Atlantic Ocean to the Mississippi River.

had already won their independence from Great Britain, and the new republic was beginning to form a new constitution.

John Crockett supported his family not only by hunting but also as an elected constable in Greene Country with the power to arrest wrongdoers. In later years, Davy would similarly provide for his own family by hunting and as a politician.

The Constitution of the United States

When Davy Crockett was born, the United States was about a third the size it is today. In 1787, when he was one, delegates met in Philadelphia to draft a constitution for the United States. The fifty-five delegates decided that the country would have a president—elected every four years. He would govern the country with the help of a Congress, consisting of a House of Representatives and a Senate (which would be made up of elected men from every state) and a Supreme Court. When the delegates finished writing the constitution, thirty-nine of them agreed to sign it. Copies of the document were sent to each state to be signed by the state leaders. Two years later, when Davy was three, the Constitution became law, and a presidential election was held. **Electors** from the states cast their votes, and George Washington was elected the nation's first president.

An 1856 painting depicts George Washington showing a copy of the Constitution of the United States to the delegates of the Constitutional Convention in 1787.

Hard Times

Life on the frontier was not easy. Violence and danger were everywhere. Davy had to be tough and resilient in order to survive. Having four older brothers helped, but sometimes their adventures proved almost disastrous. Once, they decided to take their father's canoe for a trip on the river. They were unable to convince Davy to go with them, but he watched them from the shore. None of the Crockett boys knew anything about paddling a canoe, so on the fast-moving water, they quickly lost control and started drifting toward a waterfall. Watching from afar, Davy realized that his brothers could be killed. Luckily, the Crockett boys were saved by a neighbor, Amos Kendall, who just happened to be passing by. He dived into the creek and managed to pull the canoe with the frightened boys to shore.

In 1794, when Davy was around seven, his family moved a few miles away to Cove Creek, still in the state of North Carolina.

A 1997 photo shows a Tennessee gristmill from the late 1800s. It used waterpower to grind different types of grain into flour for baking bread. Crockett's father built a similar type of gristmill in North Carolina in 1794.

There, his father and a friend, Thomas Galbreath, built a gristmill, something Davy himself would also do in years to come. Milling—the grinding of grain into flour—was one of the few industries on the American frontier at the time, and many settlers saw it as an easy way to make a living. Once the mill was complete, all they had to do was charge other settlers to use it. Unfortunately, nature had other ideas. Even before the gristmill was completed, the river overflowed its banks, destroying the mill and flooding the Crocketts' log cabin.

On the frontier, whenever such a disaster occurred, it was quite common not to rebuild but to move, and that's what the Crocketts did once again. Because John Crockett held the title to some land on the road connecting Knoxville with Abingdon, Virginia, he decided to build a log cabin on it. The structure served both as the Crocketts' home and as a tavern that provided room, board, and drink for all the **wagoners** passing through what was now the new state of Tennessee. Still, Davy's father could not make enough money to pay all of his debts (some incurred because of the gristmill), and the sheriff of Jefferson County seized the property on November 4, 1795. It was later sold at public auction.

Wagoners were the "truck drivers" of early America, hauling goods all over the country. In this drawing, c. 1876, two wagoners are urging a team of horses up a steep hill.

Early-American Taverns

In colonial America, taverns were an important part of people's social lives because they were usually the only available public meeting places. Men from all over the area, from all walks of life, would meet there to discuss politics, conduct business, and eat a hearty meal, along with a glass of wine or a tankard of ale. Taverns were also a necessity for America's travelers. They were usually located every few miles on the main roads where weary men and women could get food, drink, and a bed (or a floor) for the night. Although the landlords of colonial taverns might not have been the wealthiest men in the area, they were certainly the best known and often the most popular. When travelers later wrote accounts of their journeys, they almost always mentioned the taverns where they stayed.

Early-American taverns—one of which is depicted in this c. 1820 watercolor—not only served food and drink to weary travelers but also were usually the only places in small towns for social gatherings.

Leaving Home

Davy was now old enough to be embarrassed by his family's loss of the tavern. Out of compassion but also for a percentage of the profits, William Line, the man who had bought the property, allowed the Crockett family to continue to live there and to run the tavern. Life was still hard, and everyone was expected to do his share of work to contribute to the family's livelihood.

Davy split fence rails and hunted game. Even that wasn't enough, though. In 1798, Jacob Siler, a recent immigrant from the Netherlands, stopped by the tavern. He was on his way to Rockbridge, Virginia, with a herd of cattle, and John Crockett offered to let Siler take Davy along to help him—for a price. Although twelve-year-old Davy was scared at the thought of leaving home, what absolutely terrified him was knowing that when the journey was over, he would be expected to return to Tennessee by himself. Still, he knew the decision wasn't up to him, so he remained silent and obeyed. "[Davy is] not unlike a [boy] from the [Netherlands]," Siler told Davy's father, "mindful of his elders and obedient. And he sits at your feet and listens and learns."

The four-hundred-mile trip took more than two weeks. To Davy, it seemed much longer. He was very unhappy most of the time—except when Siler let him shoot his German-made rifle. This allowed Davy to show off his hunting skills and to supply the **drovers** with fresh meat. When they finally reached Virginia, Siler gave Davy several dollars to keep for himself, even though he had already paid Davy's father for the boy's work. To Davy's surprise, Siler also

> *He was very unhappy most of the time—except when Siler let him shoot his German-made rifle.*

suggested that Davy stay on in Virginia and continue to work for him. Even though Davy was homesick, he agreed. On the outside, he acted happy about his decision. "I got the family all to believe I was fully satisfied." On the inside, though, he was still miserable.

Cattle drives were very much a part of the landscape during Davy Crockett's time. Here, drovers lead an almost endless herd of livestock along a road to market.

Back to Tennessee

Davy stayed with the Siler family for only a month, all the time acting happy to be with them but deep inside trying to figure out a way to return to Tennessee. It finally came one Sunday night during a snowstorm. There was a tavern near the Siler's home. Davy had been to it many times and had listened to the familiar tales of the wagoners. He knew that two of them were planning to be there that night. Davy had made prior arrangements with them to travel to Tennessee. Before Davy went to bed, he packed his belongings and waited for hours until he felt he could leave the Siler's house without being noticed.

From the tavern, Davy traveled several miles with the men, but their wagons were so slow that he got impatient and set off alone on foot. It was not long, though, before a man on horseback, leading several horses behind him, stopped and asked Davy if he would like to ride one of the horses. Davy readily agreed. Now the trip went faster, and in a few days, when Davy and the man parted company, he was just a few miles from his father's tavern.

When Davy arrived home, his family was happy to see him, and he felt older than he was. He had seen the world beyond Jefferson County, and he knew things that the people around him didn't. Still, that wasn't enough for John Crockett. He wanted Davy to go to school. He wanted his sons to have a *formal* education. Davy really wasn't very interested in that.

In frontier America, schools were set up by citizens who were considered leaders in their communities. John Crockett had once been a constable, so he, along with other prominent men in the area, hired Benjamin Kitchen to start a school nearby. It was only natural, then, that the elder Crockett would want his sons to attend.

School Days

That autumn of 1799, thirteen-year-old Davy Crockett started school. Unfortunately, he had only just begun to learn the alphabet when he had a fight with the school bully, but Davy wasn't about to let someone more powerful get the best of him. This was a trait that would surface again and again for the rest of his life. "I scratched his face all [over], and soon made him cry

Unlike today's fully equipped modern schools, America's early frontier schools were stark places. When students misbehaved—like Davy—they were usually switched or caned by the teacher.

out for [mercy]." After the fight, though, Davy convinced himself that Mr. Kitchen was going to give him a whipping because of it.

The following day, Davy left for school as usual, but along the way he decided to hide out in the woods instead. He also managed to convince his brothers not to tell their father on him. After school, Davy's brothers would call to him, and they would all walk home together. Finally, though, after this had gone on for several days, Mr. Kitchen sent a note home asking where Davy was. Mr. Crockett confronted Davy, and Davy told him the truth—that he was afraid Mr. Kitchen would whip him because of the fight. This time, Mr. Crockett said he would only give Davy a warning, but if it happened again, he could certainly expect a whipping at home.

The next day, Davy did head off to school, but he wasn't walking fast enough for his father, who took off after him with a hickory switch (a common form of punishment for the time). "[He had been] taking a few horns [of whiskey] and was in a good condition to make the fur fly." Davy ran. His father was fast, but Davy was faster. Now, Davy decided, there was only one solution to his predicament. He would run away to keep from being whipped at home by his father and at school by Mr. Kitchen.

Running Away from Home

Davy had only gone a mile down the road when he suddenly remembered that his older brother, John, had signed on with a neighbor, Jesse Cheek, to help him drive a herd of cattle to Virginia, so he asked Cheek for a job, too. Cheek was glad to have Davy with him because he knew Davy was a hard worker. Neither Cheek nor Davy's brother asked him about missing school.

To Davy, the trip was an easy one because he had already traveled the road to Abingdon on his first cattle drive with Jacob Siler. This time, though, the cattle drive took Davy farther east into Virginia—to Lynchburg, and then on to Charlottesville, the home of then Vice President Thomas Jefferson. During the drive, Davy occasionally admitted to being homesick, but he also liked being able to make his own decisions about what would happen next in his life. The drive finally ended at Front Royal, Virginia, where the cattle were sold. Perhaps, Davy thought, it was time to return home.

CHAPTER 2

A Difficult Journey Home

I often thought of home, and, indeed, wished bad enough to be there, [but I also remembered] my father, and the big hickory he carried.

When Cheek's brother offered to share his horse and return with him to Tennessee, Davy accepted his offer and said good-bye to his own brother. After a few days, though, Davy realized that there wasn't much sharing, because Cheek seemed to be doing all the riding. Davy told the man that he'd find his own way back to Tennessee. They agreed to part company, and Cheek gave Davy four dollars to help him with his food and lodging.

Traveling to Gerrardstown, Virginia

With his personable and gregarious nature, it was easy for Davy to befriend other travelers on the busy road. It wasn't long before he met up with Adam Myers, a wagoner traveling north from Tennessee. Myers asked Davy to accompany him back north to Gerrardstown, Virginia, to help him deliver the goods in his wagon, and then Davy could ride back with him to Tennessee. As much as Davy wanted to return home, he had already talked himself into believing that his father would be waiting for him with a switch. "I often thought of home, and, indeed, wished bad enough to be there, [but I also remembered] my father, and the big hickory he carried." Davy agreed to go with Myers.

When Davy and Myers reached Gerrardstown, they unloaded Myers's wagon, but Myers was told that he would have to go on north to Alexandria, on the Potomac River, to pick up a return load. Davy stayed behind and worked for John Gray, a local farmer, for twenty-five cents a day.

Upon Myers's return, he told Davy that he wouldn't be going back to Tennessee after all because he could make more money with regular runs between Gerrardstown and Baltimore, Maryland, just north of Washington, D.C. Somewhat disappointed, Davy told himself it was for the best and continued to work for John Gray. However, in the spring of 1800, Davy decided to accompany Myers to Baltimore. He gave the man his life savings of seven dollars for safekeeping.

An Offer to Go to Sea

Baltimore was a revelation to Davy. He had never seen a real city before. He had also never seen sailing ships, and there were

Baltimore was one of America's most important ports during Crockett's time. When visiting the city for the first time, he might have seen a vista of Baltimore like the one seen from Federal Hill in this c. 1831 print.

several tied up in Baltimore Harbor. Davy went on board one of the ships and met the captain. Again, because of Davy's friendly nature, the captain offered Davy a job. The ship was sailing for England in a few days, and the captain thought that Davy would make an excellent sailor. Young Crockett was physically fit, and he wasn't so tall that he'd be uncomfortable in the cramped lower decks. His outgoing personality would also be welcomed by the rest of the crew during long weeks at sea. Davy accepted the captain's offer.

To Davy's surprise, Myers refused to return Davy's seven dollars or any of his belongings and even threatened to punish Davy if he tried to leave. Davy couldn't believe it. He had always expected men to keep their promises to him, at least as best they could. Obviously, Myers was a man whose word meant nothing to him—a trait that was loathsome to Davy.

He had always expected men to keep their promises to him, at least as best they could.

On the trip from Baltimore back to Gerrardstown, Davy felt like a prisoner. He finally did escape while Myers was asleep— but only with his clothes, and without his seven dollars. Once again, Davy met someone on the road who agreed to help him. The man's name was Myers, too. At first this made Davy suspicious, but the man explained that he was *Henry* Myers, from Pennsylvania, and was absolutely no relation to *Adam* Myers.

Davy stayed with his new friend for a couple of days, then decided that he would try to get back to Tennessee on his own. Henry Myers told several other wagoners of Davy's plight, and the men took up a collection for Davy. The next morning, he set out for Tennessee with three dollars in his pocket. He was a happy young man.

Eighteenth-Century Sailing Ships

Eighteenth-century sailing ships carried the world's richest cargoes, such as tea, spices, furniture, and jewelry. Because these cargoes were worth a lot of money, the ships were outfitted with at least fifty cannons to defend against pirates. The captain had a private cabin, where he slept, organized his charts, and ate with his officers. His officers had to share cabins. Ordinary sailors slept in **hammocks** and were only allowed a space about fourteen inches wide per man. Usually there were chickens, goats, and sheep aboard, and it wasn't unusual for cattle to be kept in the lower deck area. Meat from these animals was used to supplement the other food, such as hard biscuits and salted beef, but they were only slaughtered on special occasions or when needed to keep the men from starving. Gunpowder was stored below the waterline and kept safe from sparks by felt door flaps soaked in water. When sailors went to the toilet, they used planks with holes situated over the water.

Hundreds of merchant ships, like this British East Indiaman, sailed the seas in the 1800s, carrying goods to and from the United States.

More Money Problems

Unfortunately, the money did not take him as far as he had hoped. When Davy reached the Roanoke River, he was out of money. After working on a farm for a month, he **indentured** himself for four years to a hatmaker who promised to teach him the trade. However, the job only lasted eighteen months before the hatmaker went out of business and left without paying any of his employees, Davy included.

In early America, wealthy men had their hats specially made by "hatters." In this 1867 drawing, a man tries on a top hat for the proper fit. As a young boy, Crockett hoped to learn the trade.

Once again, Davy was alone, penniless, and several hundred miles from Tennessee. There was nothing else to do except find whatever odd jobs were available in the area. Finally, he had saved up enough money to buy himself some new clothes and to have some left for food while he made the rest of the trip back home.

Davy had only gone a few miles, though, when he reached the New River, which was about to flood because of the recent heavy rains. He needed to cross the river, but the ferry wasn't operating. Undeterred, Davy found an abandoned canoe and set off by himself, but the strong current and cold wind carried him several miles downstream before he finally made it to the other side. Davy was soaked to the skin, and his clothing was beginning to freeze. "A mighty ticklish business, I tell you," he later described when relating this experience.

Finally Making It Home

Davy finally made it to a tavern, where he was able to sit close to the fire so he could both warm up and dry his clothing. The tavern owner also gave him a tankard of ale. With dry clothes and a renewed spirit of determination, Davy thanked the kind owner for his hospitality and headed out on the road toward Tennessee.

It was well after dark when Davy reached the Crocketts' tavern. After all this time, he wondered what his reception would be. He quietly entered and sat down alongside some of the other travelers. He said nothing. He just listened. Finally, his sister Betsy looked at him, and her face burst into a smile. Someone had recognized him at last.

Everyone was delighted to see Davy, including his father, who never mentioned the hickory switch. He did let Davy know, though, that he still expected him to be a dutiful son and to obey one last request.

An Honorable Debtor

While Davy was gone, his father had accumulated a debt of thirty-six dollars (about 415 dollars by today's standards) with a

Money in Colonial America

During America's colonial period, all the states suffered from a lack of official coins to carry out normal trade. In North Carolina in 1775, there were at least seventeen different forms of money, all of which had been declared **legal tender**.

Colonial money included:
- the scarce but official British coinage of pounds, shillings, and pence, based on the **imperial system.**
- paper money, produced by the different states.
- unofficial coinage, especially that of Spain and Portugal.
- traditional Native American currencies, such as furs and **wampum**.
- the so-called "country money" such as tobacco, rice, and wheat.

When the Revolutionary War started in 1776, the American Congress decided to finance it by using an almost overwhelming supply of its paper money called Continentals. By the end of the war in 1783, the value of a Continental had fallen to 1/1,000 of its original value, giving rise to the phrase still used today, "not worth a Continental."

This Continental banknote was worth twenty dollars in 1778. When paper money came into use, governments tried to support their paper currency with equal amounts of precious metals, especially gold.

man named Abraham Wilson. Mr. Crockett wanted Davy to work for Wilson and repay the debt. Davy agreed, and he spent the next six months of 1802 doing various odd jobs until his father's debt was paid.

Davy disliked working for Wilson and declined the man's offer of more work. Instead, Davy took a job with John Kennedy, a Quaker, in hopes of earning his own money. At the end of his first week of work, though, Kennedy told Davy that John Crockett also owed him forty dollars. A stunned Davy agreed to use his earnings to pay off that debt, too.

Mr. Crockett wanted Davy to work for Wilson and repay the debt.

When Davy finally returned home, after not seeing his parents while he was working for Kennedy, he presented his father with a forty-dollar note that was paid in full. At first, Davy's father thought Kennedy had sent Davy to collect the money, but Davy told him that he had worked off the debt and that the paid note was a present. At that, John Crockett "shed a heap of tears."

The next day, Davy returned to the Kennedy's to begin working for himself. Although he had already worked there a year, he had not accumulated any of his own money.

CHAPTER 3

Courtin' and Marriage

Having gotten my wife, I thought I . . . needed nothing more in the whole world. But I soon found this was all a mistake—for now . . . I had nothing to give for [her].

rockett had now been working for John Kennedy for two months, earning money for himself. His life seemed to be on track again. Then Kennedy's niece, Linda Kennedy from North Carolina, paid the family a visit, and Crockett's world was turned upside down. He had never seen such a beautiful girl before. "I thought that if all the hills about were pure chink [metal], and all belonged to me, I would give them if I could just talk to her as I wanted to."

After admiring her from afar, Crockett finally managed to get up enough courage to tell the young lady that he wanted to marry her and that if she refused him he would probably die. Gently, Kennedy's niece told him that she was already engaged to one of Kennedy's sons. Crockett was devastated. In fact, he convinced himself that the real reason for this rejection was that he was not educated like the Kennedy boys.

Getting an Education

Crockett knew that another one of John Kennedy's sons had started a school nearby, so he struck a bargain with the young man. Davy would work for him a couple of days a week, doing various chores, in exchange for being allowed to attend his class. The young Kennedy agreed.

Unlike Crockett's previous experience with school, this one was different because he wanted to be there. He wanted to learn everything he could. It wasn't long before he had mastered the alphabet and was soon reading and doing arithmetic. After six months, Crockett was considered a **literate** man, well ahead of the other students his own age in learning "to read a little in my primer, to write my own name, and to [calculate] some in the three first rules of figures."

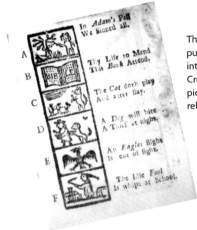

The *New England Primer* was first published in Boston around 1688 and introduced colonial children like Davy Crockett to their ABCs by means of pictures and rhymes—mostly of a religious nature.

Trying to Find a Wife

Now Crockett was nineteen years old and knew he could continue his education on his own, so he stopped attending school. He remembered how happy he was when he was in love with Linda Kennedy, so he started looking around for a woman who could become his wife.

Frontier Schools

In Colonial America, wealthy families hired tutors and governesses to teach their children. Sometimes, they sent their sons to private schools. On America's frontier, though, children seldom went to school, and if they did, it was only for a few years, because as soon as they could work, they were needed at home. The frontier schools were usually log cabins, twelve feet by sixteen feet, with a window at each end of the building. Often, there were no more than twelve seats, a teacher's desk, and a bench at the front of the room where pupils went to recite their lessons. At night and on Saturdays, the buildings were often used for such social events as debates, spelling bees, and traveling theater groups.

School buildings on America's frontier were usually one-room log cabins, built from the timber of surrounding trees. This old log cabin schoolhouse in Tennessee, located next to a deteriorating cemetery, was photographed in 1983.

Crockett remembered a family from his childhood, the Elders, who had several daughters. He decided to pay them a visit. Although they were all of marriageable age now, and most of them were quite pretty, Crockett decided that Margaret would make the best bride. He asked if he could court her, and Margaret agreed. The courtship mostly consisted of a few visits to the Elders's home. Crockett, remembering what had happened

So, in October 1805, nineteen-year-old Crockett appeared before the court clerk . . . and applied for a marriage license.

with Linda Kennedy, wanted to get married as soon as possible. So, in October 1805, nineteen-year-old Crockett appeared before the court clerk in Dandridge in Jefferson County and applied for a marriage license. He could hardly contain his happiness.

Crockett later entered a shooting contest and shot well enough with his new rifle to win a whole side of beef, which he sold for five dollars. He felt he could use the money to start his marriage. Besides, fowl and game were plentiful in the woods for hunting, but money was not.

With the money in hand, Crockett started toward the Elders's house. Before he reached it, though, he met one of Margaret's sisters who told him that Margaret had decided she didn't want to marry Crockett after all. The sister added tearfully that Margaret already had plans to marry someone else and that Margaret had just been playing a prank on him all along.

Crockett was thunderstruck. For a few minutes, his brain wouldn't accept what he had just heard, but Margaret's sister assured him that she was telling the truth. Now, he was thoroughly convinced—as he had thought years before—that he had been born for hardships, misery, and disappointments. "It was the worst kind of sickness, a sickness of the heart."

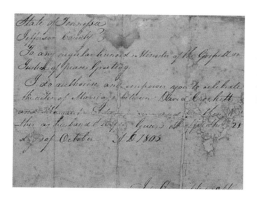

With high hopes of marrying Margaret Elders, Davy Crockett prematurely signed this October 1805 marriage contract. Alas, Miss Elders changed her mind and married someone else.

Within a month, though, Crockett decided that what happened was probably for the best. He started thinking again of how he could find a wife but avoid the misery that had befallen him before.

One of the Kennedy brothers told him about a frolic, a type of party that was to be held that night at a neighbor's barn. Crockett knew that there was a lot of singing, dancing, and drinking—as well as pretty girls—at these frolics, but he had never felt comfortable attending them. Still, if this was where the eligible young ladies were, then this was where he should be, too.

Courtship and Marriage

Crockett didn't meet anyone he was interested in at the first two frolics he attended, but at the next one he met Polly Finley— a young woman he wanted for his wife. This time, Davy not only courted Polly, but he also tried to court her mother as well. He thought that if he won her mother's approval, it would be difficult for Polly to turn him down. Unfortunately, Mrs. Finley was not taken with Davy, and he told his friends that when Mrs. Finley looked at him, she was "as savage as a meat ax," meaning her face was really scary!

Frolics

From time to time, settlers living on America's colonial frontier would have parties called frolics. Often, a young man went to these frolics to find a wife. Although it could take several frolics before some suitable girl caught a young man's eye, he was almost always successful.

A frolic could be any type of get-together that brought in people from miles around to enjoy each other's company. The celebration often lasted for several days. Sometimes these activities included reapings (harvestings), house raisings, and quilting bees. However, more often the frolics were more about drinking and gambling, dogfights and cockfights, horse racing, shooting matches, log rolling, and arguing about politics—almost anything that those gathered considered entertaining. Of course, there was also dancing, usually to music from homemade fiddles.

American settlers always managed to find some time once or twice a month for a frolic. This 18th-century painting depicts an outdoor frolic.

Crockett also had a rival—another young man who had set his eyes on Polly as a bride—but Davy vowed not to give up. In time, it was Crockett who won Polly's heart, and eventually, using his charm, he also won over Mrs. Finley.

At the beginning of August 1806, Davy Crockett, now almost twenty years old, once again went to the clerk court's office in Dandridge and took out a marriage license. A few days later, in the frontier custom of the time, he sent a group of friends with an empty jug to the Finley house. If Mr. Finley filled it with liquor, he was telling Crockett that he would welcome Crockett as a son-in-law, and his marriage to Polly could proceed. When Crockett finally saw his friends returning, he held his breath until they got close enough so that he could see the contents of the jug were sloshing over the rim!

Davy was ecstatic, and he immediately sent one of his friends to get a preacher. The wedding ceremony took place at the Finley home on August 14, but the wedding party afterward was held at the Crocketts' tavern. A large plank table was covered with pork, venison, wild turkey, and bear meat alongside cornbread and potatoes. Black slaves strummed banjoes, played fiddles, and rattled bones. Everyone present ate and danced until almost dawn.

A frontier jug was an earthenware container that was used to store liquids, especially spirits such as whiskey. To Crockett, a filled jug meant his future in-laws had accepted him into the family.

Colonial weddings were truly special events, as shown in this undated illustration. Like Davy and Polly's wedding, the guests all ate and danced until the sun came up the next morning.

During the first days of their marriage, Crockett and his new wife lived with her parents, but then, with two cows and two calves as a wedding gift, they moved into a small rented farm nearby and began their married life together. It didn't take Davy long to realize what an awesome responsibility marriage was. He was suddenly aware that he really had nothing more to offer her than himself, but he vowed that he would be the best husband a woman could ever want.

Their first child, John Wesley, was born on July 10, 1807, and two years later a second son, William, was added to the family. While Crockett had no trouble feeding his family by hunting, there was never enough money to pay the rent or to get anything else his family might want. When frontier families found themselves in this kind of situation, they usually moved westward—even if only by a few miles. There was always the feeling that things would be better down the road.

Frontier families often dealt with hardships such as floods, unproductive land, and unwanted neighbors by moving farther west. This undated illustration shows one such family searching for a "better" place to live.

An Unsuccessful Homesteader

The Crocketts moved twice during the next four years. In 1811, they traveled more than 150 miles, past Knoxville and south to Lincoln County to a spot on Mulberry Creek, where Crockett entered a claim as a **homesteader** for a five-acre site and built a log cabin. In those days, if a person farmed the land for a few months, he could receive legal title to it, but he would still have to pay the taxes on it. Once again, though, Crockett couldn't seem to succeed.

Instead of doing what other homesteaders did—planting crops and building fences to keep some cows—he spent most of his time doing what he liked best: hunting deer and other game. After all, the hunting there was much better than any place he had ever been. Polly never complained, though, and continued to make them a pleasant home using only the meager things that were given to her by family and friends.

On November 25, 1812, a daughter, Margaret, was born. With his family increasing, Crockett knew he had to become a better provider. He convinced himself that he would be more successful if he had more land, so he entered a claim for fifteen nearby acres. By the time his claim was accepted, however, Crockett had already moved his family again a few miles farther south, to nearby Franklin County on Bean's Creek, almost on the Alabama border. In doing so, Crockett had taken his family to a part of the state that was still considered Indian country.

With his family increasing, Crockett knew he had to become a better provider.

When Davy Crockett took his family to a new homestead, he and his sons first built the cabin in which they would live, then, instead of clearing the land for crops, Davy headed off into the woods to hunt, much like the men depicted in this c. 1867 lithograph.

CHAPTER 4

A Scout and Indian Fighter

The enemy fought with savage fury, and met death with all its [horrors], without shrinking or complaining: not one asked to be spared, but fought as long as they could stand or sit.

In 1812, the United States was at war with Great Britain again. The British had discovered willing allies among the southeastern Native American tribes—especially the Creeks—and were arming them to fight the American settlers there. On August 30, 1813, a band of Creek warriors attacked some white settlers and two companies of Mississippi Volunteer soldiers who had taken refuge at Fort Mims, a **stockade** about thirty miles from Mobile on

A c. 1874 illustration depicts the massacre at Fort Mims in the Alabama Territory on August 30, 1813. A band of Creeks is shown attacking white settlers in retaliation for an earlier attack by whites on a Creek hunting party.

The Creek Nation

Until the middle of the 1500s, the Creek nation controlled almost all of what is today the state of Georgia, but by the 1600s, after battles with other nations, the Creeks eventually settled south of the Chattahoochee and Flint Rivers and west to the Coosa River in Alabama. During the American Revolution, the Creek nation was mostly neutral, but some factions fought for the British and some fought for the Americans.

After the war, relations between the state of Georgia and the Creek nation worsened. The Creeks declared war in 1798 and attacked settlers living on Creek land. During the War of 1812, the Shawnee warrior Tecumseh rallied the Red Sticks—full-blooded Creeks—to attack the settlers, but General Andrew Jackson eventually defeated the Creeks. The entire Creek nation was forced to surrender one-third of its land to the United States.

By 1827, Georgians had succeeded in removing the entire Creek nation from their state. The Creeks had been forced off all their land and had begun following the other southeastern Native Americans along the Trail of Tears toward what was now Indian Territory—the eastern part of the present state of Oklahoma.

By 1827, Georgia had succeeded in removing the entire Creek nation from their state, forcing them to follow what would soon be known as the Trail of Tears in 1838—depicted here in a 1942 painting by Robert Lindneux.

the Alabama River. The attack was in retaliation for one earlier in the summer when some settlers attacked a party of Creeks at Burnt Corn Creek in the southern part of Alabama Territory.

When the fighting was finally over, almost five hundred settlers and soldiers were dead, but about fifty people had escaped, and they spread the news of the attack throughout the rest of the area. The American settlers were in shock. Although the British army was hundreds of miles away, their allies, the Creeks, were not; and everyone knew now that the war had suddenly appeared on their doorstep.

Off to War

When Davy heard the news, he told Polly that it was his duty to join the local **militia** and to fight the Creeks. Crockett was by nature even tempered. He was really more interested in having fun and hunting in the woods than he was in fighting other men, but he saw this as a question of defending what he considered his right to live in peace in a land in which there was plenty of room for everyone. Later, in his autobiography, published in 1834, he would say, "I . . . had often thought about war, and I . . . believe[d] . . . that I couldn't fight in that way at all."

For several days, Polly pleaded with Crockett not to leave. She didn't know how she could survive in an area that still seemed so strange to her, far away from family and friends, and with young children to take care of. Crockett tried to get Polly to see that it was his responsibility. In the end, Polly was more resigned than accepting. Early on the morning of September 24, Crockett picked up his rifle, mounted his horse, and rode to Winchester, about ten miles away, where the other volunteers had gathered.

Under Captain Francis Jones, Crockett enlisted to serve for ninety days as part of the Second Regiment of Tennessee

Volunteers. Now that he knew how long he'd be gone, he returned home to his family, where he spent a couple of days chopping enough firewood and hunting and butchering enough game that Polly and the children could survive until he returned.

When Crockett and the other volunteers crossed into Alabama Territory, they were all glad to be among the first men to fight in what became known as the Creek War, which was part of the larger War of 1812. They first headed for Beaty's Spring, just a few miles beyond Huntsville, Alabama. There, they met several other companies of militia until their number reached almost 1,300 men, all now under the command of Colonel John Coffee, a close friend of the overall commander, General Andrew Jackson.

The massacre at Fort Dearborn, shown in this 19th-century wood engraving, was one of the many Native American attacks in the Creek War, which was fought during the War of 1812.

Leading a Scouting Party

Colonel Coffee needed two men for a scouting expedition. They should be the best woodsmen and riflemen among all the militia gathered. Captain Jones said there was none better than Davy Crockett, who was then asked to find a second man to accompany him. When Crockett chose George Russell, who was a family friend from Franklin Country but barely old enough even to be in the militia, Captain Jones was displeased. Crockett assured him that George was the measure of any man there. Captain Jones, needing Crockett's skills, accepted George grudgingly.

Captain Jones said there was none better than Davy Crockett . . .

The expedition, which also included Major John H. Gibson and several other men, set off to find the houses of two Cherokee leaders, Dick Brown and his father. These men were rivals of the Creeks, and Crockett hoped they could gather some intelligence on what the Creeks were planning to do.

At Ditto's Landing the expedition split up, one group under Major Gibson, the other under Crockett. They agreed to meet later that evening at a crossroads beyond Dick Brown's house. Unfortunately, Crockett was unable to get any useful information from the Cherokees. When he and his men arrived back at the crossroads, Major Gibson and his group weren't there.

The next morning, Major Gibson and his men still hadn't shown up. Crockett decided to take his group to a Cherokee village on the border of the Creek nation, twenty miles away, near the Georgia border. Although Cherokees did not consider themselves enemies of Creeks, they also did not support the Creeks' war efforts, so Crockett thought he might have some success in learning from them exactly what the Creeks planned to do.

On the way, they stopped at the home of a white man named Radcliff who was married to a Creek woman. Crockett asked Radcliff if he had seen any Creek warriors in the area. The man was so nervous that he could hardly speak, but he managed to tell Crockett that a band of Red Sticks had passed by his house in war paint less than an hour before. Red Sticks were full-blooded Creeks who hated the American settlers for taking their lands. They were known by this colorful name because the clubs they carried were often covered with blood.

Now some of Crockett's men started to get nervous about confronting the Creeks in battle. A few of them even suggested that they should all return to Beaty's Creek, but Crockett told them, "The first man who turns his horse north will get a rifle ball between his shoulders."

Radcliff also told Crockett that some friendly Creeks were camped only a few miles away and might be able to give him more information on the war party. These Creeks—many of whom had intermarried with white settlers—had adopted the settlers' way of life and were also despised by the Red Sticks. Crockett and his men headed for the camp.

The Creeks, as depicted in this undated woodcut, were a powerful southeastern American Indian tribe. During the War of 1812, pure-blood Creeks, called Red Sticks, were allied with the British and fought against the Creeks who had intermarried with white settlers and had adopted their ways.

Before Crockett and his men reached the camp, they met two black men who were runaway slaves. Ironically, they had escaped from their Creek captors and were trying to get back to their white owners. Crockett asked one of the men who could speak Creek to go with him to the Creek camp, and he let the other man continue on his way.

At the camp, a friendly Creek told Crockett that if the Red Sticks found Crockett and his men there, the whole camp would be wiped out. Crockett assured the man that he would make moccasins out of the skins of any Red Sticks who dared to attack the camp. This reassured the friendly Creek somewhat. But when a friendly Creek messenger later roused the sleeping camp with the news that the Red Sticks had crossed the Coosa River in Alabama and were headed toward General Andrew Jackson's force, Crockett knew he had to warn them. He and his men set off right away for Ditto's Landing, which was sixty-five miles away.

After several hours of hard riding, Crockett and his men finally reached the camp, and Crockett reported the information to Colonel Coffee. Instead of assembling his troops into action, as Crockett expected, Coffee merely posted a double guard that night. Crockett wondered why such little action was taken. However, when Major Gibson returned the next day with the same information, Colonel Coffee immediately ordered his men to build fortifications. Crockett was furious and began "burning inside like a tar kiln." He decided that his report wasn't believed because he wasn't an officer—"just a poor soldier."

A Bloody Battle

When General Jackson received the news, he mobilized his troops to confront the Creeks headed their way. It was soon learned, though, that the Creek messenger who had delivered the

A lithograph published between 1834 and 1845 shows General Andrew Jackson with Tennessee forces after defeating the Red Stick Creeks in the War of 1812.

warning about the Red Sticks had actually been sent by Radcliff as a prank to get the militia away from his property.

Nevertheless, Coffee, who had been promoted to brigadier general a few days earlier, decided to march his troops to Ten Islands, Alabama. There, he set up a camp and named it Fort Strother. Within days, Coffee's scouts learned that a band of almost three hundred Creeks was encamped at Tallussahatchee, about ten miles away. Coffee and his men surrounded the camp. A few **volleys** were exchanged before most of the Creeks surrendered, realizing that a fight was hopeless. However, about forty-six Creeks took refuge in one house, vowing to fight to the death.

As some of the militiamen approached the house, a Creek woman shot an arrow, killing a lieutenant next to Crockett. He was stunned. He had never seen a man killed before. Now the volunteers wanted revenge. They riddled the Creek woman with bullets, then began firing a hail of bullets at the warriors. Finally, the volunteers got close enough to the house to set it on fire. Rather than surrender, the Creek warriors burned to death. General Jackson said the victory at Tallussahatchee had righted the wrong of Fort Mims.

A Short Break from the War

With winter approaching and with food scarce, the volunteers wanted to go home. General Jackson was opposed to this, but finally relented, thinking that the men would simply disobey his orders and leave anyway. He told them, however, they all had to return to Huntsville by December 8.

Polly and the children were overjoyed when they saw Crockett, but Polly's joy soon turned to anger when she learned that her husband would only be home for two weeks. During that time, Crockett chopped more wood and shot more game for his family; then he returned to fulfill the rest of his enlistment. Some of the other volunteers didn't.

Crockett was back home by Christmas, though, having completed his service honorably. Nevertheless, in January of 1814, Crockett left home again to continue fighting the Creeks with General Jackson. At the Battle of Horseshoe Bend on March 28, the Creeks were finally defeated, and, once again, Crockett returned home. However, there are no military records that show Crockett had actually participated in this conflict.

When the British army burned Washington, D.C., in August of that year as part of the continuing War of 1812, Crockett reenlisted, because he now wanted to fight the British directly. Polly was dismayed, but she knew there was nothing she could do to keep him from leaving again.

This c. 1814 drawing shows the burned-out shell of the Capitol in Washington, D.C., after British troops set fire to it in August 1814.

Fighting in Florida

Crockett, now a sergeant, was sent to Florida with the Tennessee Mounted Gunmen. Even though Spain controlled the territory, the British were using the city of Pensacola for their naval base. By the time the Tennesseans arrived, though, the British had abandoned the city.

The rest of 1814 proved more difficult for the mounted gunmen. Much of their time was spent chasing small bands of Seminoles through the Florida swamps. Remembering when their provisions began to run out, Crockett later wrote, "We all began to get nearly ready to give up the ghost, and lie down and die, for we had no prospect of provision, and we knew we couldn't go much further without it." In spite of their dire situation, Crockett saved the troops from starvation by using his

Kentucky Long Rifle to hunt and supply the men with enough meat to keep them alive. It wasn't the first or last time that his trusty rifle would save lives.

Early in 1815, word reached Crockett that Polly was sick. By riding day and night, he managed to make it back home within just a few weeks. Polly died not long afterward of an unknown illness, and Crockett was almost inconsolable. He blamed himself and his long absences for her death.

When it was time for Crockett to return to the Tennessee Mounted Gunmen, he knew he couldn't go. There was no one to take care of his children. As was common practice at that time, he paid a young man to take his place, and no one thought any less of him for doing it.

Davy Crockett and the Tennessee Mounted Gunmen spent much of 1814 chasing Seminoles through the swamps of Spanish-occupied Florida. This c. 1842 lithograph shows a Seminole leader.

Kentucky Long Rifles

The first Kentucky Long Rifle was actually made in Lancaster, Pennsylvania, sometime in the 1730s, by a German immigrant. With narrower and longer barrels, these single-shot rifles were deadly at more than 200 yards, an astonishing range at that time. They were the primary weapon of the frontiersmen, especially in Kentucky and Tennessee.

During the American Revolution, George Washington made a special effort to recruit men who owned such rifles. These men were used mostly as snipers to pick off British soldiers. Because men who owned a Kentucky Long Rifle usually wore buckskins— clothing made from the skins of the male deer—British soldiers soon steered clear of *anyone* dressed that way, whether they could see the man's weapon or not. Soon, many men, no matter what kind of weapon they owned, started dressing in buckskins to fool the enemy.

Frontiersmen, such as the one depicted in this 1867 wood engraving, dressed in buckskins and carried long rifles. During the War of 1812, British soldiers feared them and steered clear of anyone who was dressed in this manner.

CHAPTER 5

A Man of Substance

*Death, that cruel [leveler] of all distinctions . . .
entered my humble cottage, and tore from my
children an affectionate good mother, and from
me a tender and loving wife.*

Davy Crockett was now a widower, a role he never
expected to play. He had three small children, a farm to
take care of, and his almost unbearable loneliness to
contend with. For one of the first times in his life, he had
absolutely no idea how to deal with his problems, but
then a possible solution came to him.

He paid a visit to his older brother
John who had also just arrived home
from the war and lived nearby. Within
days, John and his wife moved in with
Davy and took over the household
responsibilities and the rearing of his children. Meanwhile,
a still grief-stricken Crockett tried to decide what to do
with his life now that he was no longer a soldier.

*Davy Crockett was
now a widower, a
role he never
expected to play.*

Crockett knew that John and his wife wouldn't want
to stay with him forever. He needed a new wife, not only
to rear his children, but also to share her life with him.
Within a few days, he began courting Elizabeth Patton, a
widow with two young children of her own.

To Crockett, Elizabeth seemed perfect. She was from
a prominent North Carolina family, and she had a sense

of humor. She was a "good, industrious woman, and owned a snug little farm, and lived quite comfortable." Elizabeth must have thought Crockett would make a good husband and a father to her children, because she moved into his home. They were later married in May 1816, and their first child together—Robert Patton Crockett—was born on September 16.

Looking for New Land

Soon, though, Crockett began to tire of his farm on Bean's Creek. He had decided that the land wasn't very productive. Leaving his family behind, he and three friends set out that fall to explore west of the Tennessee River to find suitable farmland. It had been taken by treaty from the Creeks as part of the settlement from the Creek War.

Right from the start, the exploring party had problems. While hunting, one of the men was bitten by a poisonous snake and was left at the home of a man Davy knew from the Creek War. Crockett and the other men went on to Tuscaloosa where

The Tennessee River, depicted in this photograph, is the largest tributary of the Ohio River. During Davy Crockett's time, much of the land along it belonged to the Creeks, but it was taken by the United States after the Creek War and opened up to American settlement.

they spent the night. When they awoke the next morning, their horses were gone. They had either been stolen, or more likely, Crockett believed, had managed to pull loose sloppily tied reins. Someone had to find them, so it was decided that Crockett would go.

For the next two days, Davy trudged through swamps, crossed creeks, and hiked over mountains, all the time carrying his heavy rifle. Just when he was about to give up, he met a man who said he had just recently seen the two animals, and if Crockett continued in the direction he was going, he would surely find them.

A Grave Illness

Crockett had walked about fifty miles without success when he saw a light coming from a cabin he was passing. As was the custom of the time, he asked if he could spend the night. He went to bed, thinking that the next morning he would continue the hunt. When he awakened, though, he had a fever and his body ached so much that he was sure he wouldn't be able to move. Still, he felt obligated to return to where he had left his friends and tell them he had been unable to find the horses.

Although Crockett traveled most of the morning, he didn't cover much distance and finally collapsed by the side of the road. Two Native Americans found him and tried feeding him some melon, but Crockett could not keep any of it down. Using sign language, the men managed to convince Crockett that if he did not get help, he would die. Crockett gave one of the men his rifle to carry, and he leaned on the other one

Using sign language, the men managed to convince Crockett that if he did not get help, he would die.

until they finally made it to a house. The owners tried to revive Crockett, giving him warm tea, but they were unsuccessful, and he spent the night delirious from fever.

The next morning, two of Crockett's neighbors from Bean's Creek, who had heard what had happened to him, took him to the camp where his two original companions were waiting anxiously. Crockett's condition was getting even worse, and all of

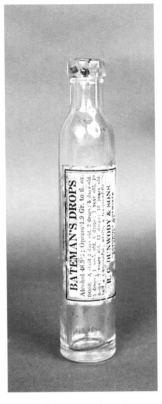

Bateman's Drops, packaged in a vial such as the one photographed here, was a medicine containing mostly alcohol and opium. In the 19th century, it was used as a cure for many illnesses.

the men thought that he would soon be dead. They took him to a nearby house and pleaded with the owners to make him as comfortable as possible before he died. They then purchased some of the owner's horses and continued their exploration of new lands without Crockett.

For almost two weeks, Crockett had a high fever and was unable to communicate with the people taking care of him. It looked like he was going to die. However, the woman living in the house refused to give up. In desperation, she gave Crockett a whole bottle of Bateman's Drops—a medicine made up of alcohol and opium. In the 1800s, it was a remedy for many illnesses, and it worked for what ailed Crockett. By the next morning, his fever had broken and he could talk. He could even take small sips of water.

Malaria

Malaria is a very serious disease that is spread by the bite of certain types of mosquitoes. It causes chills, high fever, and an enlarged **spleen**. Once a person contracts malaria, it can reoccur many times throughout that person's lifetime. Although the more common kinds of mosquitoes in the United States do not carry the **parasites** that produce malaria, swamps and other large bodies of standing, stagnant water can be breeding areas for the mosquitoes that do.

In the 1800s, malaria was known as "the ague" or "fever and ague." It was a significant barrier to the rapid settlement of the prime farmland available in the basins of America's major rivers. Sometimes, settlements along these rivers had to be abandoned after widespread outbreaks of malaria because riverboat captains refused to stop there. Today, malaria is mostly found in sub-Saharan Africa, India, Southeast Asia, the Middle East, and Central and South America, but it can also still occur in the United States.

While fighting in the swamps of Florida, Crockett was probably bitten by a mosquito carrying the parasite that causes malaria.

At the time, Crockett wasn't aware that he had malaria. He had probably contracted the disease during the Creek War when he often had to wade waist deep in the mosquito-infested swamps of west Florida looking for renegade Red Sticks and Seminoles.

When Crockett finally regained most of his strength, he was able to return home on a borrowed horse. Elizabeth thought she was seeing a ghost. Not only had Crockett lost a lot of weight while he was sick, but also his original traveling companions had returned to tell Elizabeth that her husband had died. About his appearance, Crockett later said, "I was so pale, and so much reduced, that my face looked like it had been half soled with brown paper." He was referring to the yellow-brownish paper often used on the frontier to patch holes worn into the soles of shoes.

Starting Over Again

For nearly a year after his illness, Crockett stayed home with Elizabeth and the children. He hunted and did the best he could to make his farm productive. He had almost given up the notion of finding cheap land in Alabama. However, when the Chickasaw nation surrendered some of their land in south-central Tennessee to the state, Crockett started again thinking about moving. In the summer of 1817, he left to explore the new area that the United States had finally opened up for settlement. He liked what he saw, and in the fall decided to move his family to the Shoal Creek region in Tennessee.

At that time, there was no official law enforcement in south-central Tennessee, but shortly after the Crocketts arrived, the state decreed the area a new county, and a justice of the peace— a type of law official—was needed. The residents sent in a list of the men they thought would make good justices of the peace, and Crockett's name was on it.

Initially, Davy protested, telling everyone that he knew nothing about the law. He could read and write though—unlike many of the other candidates. He also had experience in the Creek War, and he was a lieutenant in the Franklin County militia. Soon, Crockett realized that he was more than qualified to be a justice of the peace. He was elected to the office on November 25, 1817.

When Davy Crockett was a justice of the peace, he made sure people who broke the law were punished. If a man was found guilty of theft, he was whipped, much like the man in this 1883 lithograph.

Crockett did well in his new role. He used his common sense and his honesty when making decisions about the punishments for people who broke the law. He was able to make debtors pay their bills, and he made sure that men who stole were whipped. The arrest **warrants** that Crockett issued were verbal and consisted of the words, "Catch that fellow, dead or alive." As none of his rulings was ever **appealed**, he considered himself successful, even though he had never read a law book.

Becoming Colonel Crockett

Soon, Crockett was invited to run for the position of first major of the local militia, along with a Captain Matthews who would be running for the position of lieutenant colonel. Crockett hesitated at first as he considered such military ranks elitist—or snobbish. However, Matthews convinced Davy that there was not a more qualified man in the region for the job.

Matthews then invited Crockett to a frolic that he was hosting to launch their campaign. At the frolic, Davy became angry with him when he learned that Matthews's son was planning to run for first major, too. Crockett told his family that Matthews had gotten his "dander up high enough to see." He then told Matthews that he—Davy Crockett—was going to run for the position of lieutenant colonel himself.

Davy Crockett claimed that this undated portrait was the only correct likeness ever taken of him—at least up until that time.

Matthews accepted Crockett's challenge with good humor. When Crockett announced the same thing to the crowd at the frolic, they cheered him on, and on election day, March 27, 1818, Davy Crockett was elected the new lieutenant colonel of the 57th Regiment of Militia. Although Crockett only held the commission for a couple of years, he was called "colonel" for the rest of his life.

For the next few years, Crockett farmed and served in the militia. He also became one of the commissioners of Lawrenceburg, meaning he helped make decisions on how to run the town. In late 1820, Crockett was asked to run for the Tennessee state legislature, to represent Lawrence and Hickman counties. If elected, this would mean he'd be making decisions about how to run the state.

After discussing the matter with Elizabeth and the children, Crockett decided he would give it a try. On January 1, 1821, he resigned as commissioner of Lawrenceburg to start thinking about his political campaign for the Tennessee state legislature.

Crockett . . . resigned as commissioner of Lawrenceburg to start thinking about his political campaign . . .

CHAPTER 6

A Backwoods Politician

I never deceived you—I never will deceive you.

On March 1, 1821, Davy Crockett left Tennessee for North Carolina, hoping to finance his election campaign with the sale of some farm animals. However, just as he had done when he was younger, he took his time, almost unconcerned with the election, and spent almost three months away from his family, just rambling about.

On the Campaign Trail

When he returned home in June, Crockett finally threw himself into the campaign. He told the voters that he knew very little about government, which was true, but that he was honest and that he would continue to be honest if they elected him. On many subjects, Crockett refused to take a stand one way or another—a strategy that would serve him well later on.

While campaigning on the frontier, a number of candidates often spoke to one group of settlers all at the same time. At one such stop in Centerville, there was a party that lasted several days. After the hunting contests and the barbequing and the dancing were over, Crockett realized that the next thing he had to do was explain to the crowd why he would be a better **legislator** than the other candidate. Crockett, who had never made a public speech before, tried to beg off. "The thought of making a speech makes my knees feel mighty weak. You could as

well go to a pigsty for wool as to look to me for a speech." The other candidate, sensing that victory was his if the crowd saw how inept Crockett was, insisted that Crockett take first turn on the platform.

Reluctantly, Davy stood up. Once he was in front of the crowd, Crockett discovered a confidence he did not know he had. He stammered and stuttered and told all sorts of tall tales about himself. The crowds roared with laughter. They had never seen or heard anyone as natural as Davy Crockett.

At the end of his "speech," Crockett suggested that they all go over to the bar and have a drink. Almost everyone in the crowd did just that, because they wanted to hear more of what Crockett had to say—and not listen to the other candidate talk about what the government would do if they elected him. Much to Crockett's surprise, he had found just the right approach to campaigning—telling funny stories about himself and then suggesting that everyone have a drink of whiskey! It would serve him well for the rest of his political life.

That next week, though, there was a larger political gathering that was being attended by several candidates for both the governorship of Tennessee and the U.S. Congress. Crockett was unsure how his brand of humor would go over with these higher ranked politicians, but luck was with him, and he was the last one to speak. By that time, the crowd was tired of hearing speeches, so Crockett, sensing this, told one of his funny stories. He immediately won over the crowd, much to the dismay of the other candidates.

He immediately won over the crowd, much to the dismay of the other candidates.

When he left for home that evening, Crockett wasn't sure how successful he would be, but in August 1821, he won the

At the start of his campaign, Davy Crockett was unsure of his speaking ability. However, once he started telling tall tales about himself, the people loved him. Crockett is shown giving a speech in this wood engraving from a c. 1850 edition of his autobiography.

election by more than a two-to-one vote. The voters saw Crockett as a man who was one of their own. He was now a representative to the 14th Tennessee General Assembly. He was also a new father. On August 2, Elizabeth had given birth to another daughter, Matilda.

A New Tennessee Legislator

Crockett's first political assignment as a legislator came on September 17, 1821, when he became a member of the Committee of Propositions and Grievances. Now he was in a position to stand up for the rights of the men who had elected him—the poor people of western Tennessee. He could now listen to all their complaints and then propose solutions before the legislature. Fighting to make their lives better would be the major focus of the rest of his political life.

Almost immediately, Crockett became involved in trying to stop a law that would create enormous hardships for the people who had voted for him. The U.S. Congress was offering land in eastern Tennessee to veterans of the Revolutionary War, and now Congress wanted to expand those lands into western Tennessee—the district Crockett represented. He opposed this move as it meant that frontiersmen who had settled and developed the land—much like him—were in danger of being removed from it. During that first session, he voted for any law that would help western Tennessee's poor farmers and settlers and against any law that would harm them.

Fighting to make their lives better would be the major focus of the rest of his political life.

Unfortunately, before Crockett could even really settle into being a legislator, a serious problem back home almost caused him financial ruin. He had spent all of Elizabeth's money on building a gristmill on Shoal Creek. Crockett hoped that it would produce a steady income for them by grinding neighbors' grain into flour. But heavy rains on the Tennessee River flooded Shoal Creek and wiped out the operation. Now the family was not only broke, but also deeper in debt. To his relief, Elizabeth displayed no anger but only told him that they should pay off their debts as soon as possible.

When Crockett returned to the legislature in October, he continued his work on behalf of the settlers of his district. He was also becoming aware of the growing gap between the poor people of western Tennessee and the richer, more powerful residents in the central and eastern parts of the state. This gap

Even after his father's gristmill—like the one shown in this 1779 print—was destroyed by a flood, Crockett still thought that owning one was a good way to earn an income. Unfortunately, he was as unlucky in the milling business as was his father.

was also present in the legislature. Once, James C. Mitchell—who represented the richer counties in that area—insulted Crockett with what was perceived as a demeaning comment on Crockett's poor social standing. In retaliation, Crockett appeared the next day with a swatch of decorative fabric attached to his buckskin shirt. It was meant to mimic Mitchell's fancy clothes. That caused the other legislators to laugh in appreciation, but Mitchell left the chamber in anger.

The legislature adjourned in November, and Crockett returned home, with plans for a new adventure.

Gristmills

A gristmill is a building in which different kinds of grain are ground into flour. Older gristmills were powered by either water or wind. Modern mills are powered by electricity. Before the American Revolution and into the first half of the nineteenth century, gristmills provided an important service to America's farming communities. They were built and owned either individually by farmers or collectively by entire communities. Owners were paid a fee or with a percentage of the farmer's grain. By the 1850s, with railroad construction and the opening of the great grain-producing areas in the West, most local gristmills had gone out of business.

By the middle of the 19th century, railroads were being built all over the middle and western parts of the United States, forever changing the ways people traveled and goods were transported.

CHAPTER 7

Hunter and Bear Killer

There [had] been a dreadful [hurricane], which passed between [the Obion and Reelfoot Lake], and I was sure there must be a heap of bears in the fallen timber.

Once Crockett was home again, he took his oldest son, fourteen-year-old John Wesley, and a friend with him and headed west in search of better land for his family. The destruction of the gristmill and pressure from creditors had prompted Davy's decision, but his family was also growing, and he was feeling restless.

Crockett found what he was looking for on the Obion River: "There [had] been a dreadful [hurricane], which passed between [the Obion and Reelfoot Lake], and I was sure there must be a heap of bears in the fallen timber." To Crockett, it was like heaven on Earth.

Crockett knew that another family lived across the river,

Davy Crockett, portrayed in this undated woodcut, liked nothing better than hunting wild game to provide food for his family. The meat from one bear could last his family for several months.

Reelfoot Lake State Park

Reelfoot Lake State Park is located in Lake County in the northwestern corner of the state of Tennessee. The 25,000-acre lake attracts millions of visitors each year to hunt, fish, boat cruise, and watch eagles. Reelfoot Lake was formed during the New Madrid earthquake of 1811–1812. The land buckled violently, changing the landscape, reversing the flow of the Mississippi River for a time, and filling some of the land to form the lake. High winds toppled thousand of trees and created a landscape of tangled underbrush for miles around. Wildlife thrived in these conditions. Although it was hard for settlers to cross the area, hunters called it one of the best places on the frontier to find game for food—especially the black bear. Reportedly, this is the area in which Davy Crockett killed 107 bears in the fall of 1825 and the winter of 1826.

This photograph shows Reelfoot Lake State Park, which in Crockett's time was a perfect place for wild game and hunters alike.

several miles downstream, and he wanted to visit with the man. The three of them set out, undeterred by winter weather. Not only did they have to cross the river, but recent rains had also flooded much of the countryside, making travel even more difficult.

Almost half frozen, they reached the family's cabin, and the man brought out the liquor jug for Crockett and his friend while the man's wife attended to a shivering John Wesley. Also staying at the cabin were some men who were stranded when their boat full of barrels of meal, salt, and whiskey got hung up in a tangle of dead trees. They were waiting for more rain to raise the water level high enough to free the boat.

The men's destination was still a hundred miles away, north on the Obion. Crockett told them that he would supply them with enough wild game to live on for months if one of them would remain behind to help him build a cabin on his new land. The men agreed. So Crockett left them waiting for the river to rise while he went hunting.

Davy had no trouble finding game and hung his kill in the trees with plans to collect it when the men came by in their boat. He became so wrapped up in his hunting, though, that he did not realize that the river had risen high enough for the boat to clear the tangled trees. In fact, the boat had already floated past him while he had gotten lost. When the boat crew finally found Crockett—after several trips up and down the river—he was exhausted, hungry, and cold. The boatmen gave him some whiskey and wrapped him in heavy blankets.

Davy had no trouble finding game and hung his kill in the trees with plans to collect it when the men came by in their boat.

The next morning, the men collected the skinned animals and then delivered John Wesley, the friend, and Crockett back to his land. They also left one of the crewmembers there to help Davy clear the fields, build a cabin, and plant corn. When they were done, Crockett stocked enough deer and bear meat for the friend and the crewman to live on while he and John Wesley returned for the rest of the family.

When Crockett got home, there was a letter telling him that he needed to return to the state capital—which was at the time in Murfreesboro—by July 22. "I was met by an order to attend a call-session of our legislature. I attended it, and served out my time, and then returned, and took my family and what little plunder I had, and moved to where I had built my cabin, and made my [crop]."

Frozen Rivers and Gunpowder

Things started off very well for the family in their new cabin, and Crockett was able to keep them well supplied with a lot of meat. Soon, however, he ran out of gunpowder, and the heavy rains made it impossible for him to travel to Jackson, forty miles away, for a new supply. Still, Crockett had a solution to the problem. Knowing that one of Elizabeth's brothers lived south on the Obion and had a keg of powder, Crockett started out in the heavy rain to get it—against Elizabeth's advice.

In order to reach Elizabeth's brother on the opposite bank, Crockett had to cross the freezing water, which he managed to do by carefully walking on submerged logs. Still, he fell in several times, just barely keeping his rifle and spare clothes dry by holding them

Finally, he made it to his brother-in-law's house, almost dead from hypothermia . . .

The gunpowder frontiersmen used for their rifles was stored in either metal cans or wooden kegs.

over his head. Finally, he made it to his brother-in-law's house, almost dead from hypothermia, a condition of extremely low body temperature.

Crockett stayed there for almost two days, even helping to supply the family with meat, before he decided he should try to return home with the gunpowder. The river was frozen but unfortunately not to the thickness to hold a man. Halfway across, Crockett fell through the ice; still he managed to keep the powder dry. Because he had left his rifle on the bank, knowing he could not carry both it and the powder keg, he had to cross twice. Once again, he returned home to Elizabeth, almost dead from the cold.

Hunting the Biggest Black Bear

That winter, Crockett killed the biggest black bear he had ever seen. While hunting with friends, one of them spotted the immense animal. Taking careful aim with his Kentucky rifle, Crockett shot the bear twice. Instead of going down, the beast grabbed one of the hunting dogs and began mauling the poor

One winter, Davy Crockett came face-to-face with a black bear weighing more than six hundred pounds. Although he had his hatchet and knife ready, he used his rifle to kill the beast, providing enough bear meat for his family until spring of the next year.

animal. For a second, Crockett considered going after the bear with his knife and tomahawk, but he knew that the huge animal would probably claw him to death.

In order to save his dog, Crockett quickly decided to use his rifle again and hoped that he would not accidentally shoot the dog. Expert marksman that he was, Crockett fired again and finally brought the bear down. When the battle was over, Crockett quickly butchered the bear, which he was sure weighed more than six hundred pounds. His family now had enough meat to last them until spring.

In February of 1823, Crockett and John Wesley went to Jackson, Tennessee, the county seat, to trade animal skins for necessary supplies such as gunpowder, sugar, salt, and coffee. After they finished their business, Crockett decided to have a drink with some fellow volunteers from the Creek War. In the saloon were also some of the local county officials who, Crockett learned, were all candidates for the Tennessee legislature. When one of the men suggested to Crockett that he run again, he told them that although he had enjoyed standing up for the settlers of the area, he now lived too far away and that he wanted no part of government anymore. With that, Crockett and John Wesley headed home. Even though Crockett might have thought so, he was not yet done with politics.

Frontier America had abundant game with much sought-after fur. Trappers would take their bounty of otter, beaver, deer, and bear skins to trading posts, much like the one in this illustration, to exchange them for money or—more likely—for food and supplies.

CHAPTER 8

Mr. Crockett Goes to Washington

I believe the measure is unjust and wicked, and I shall fight it, let the consequences be what they may.

A few weeks after returning from Jackson, a neighbor stopped by Crockett's house and showed him an article in the county newspaper. It listed Davy Crockett as a candidate for the legislature. Crockett was furious. "I told my wife that this was all a [dirty trick] on me, but I was determined to make . . . the man who had put it there . . . [pay for] . . . the fun he [was having] at my expense."

He decided then and there that he was going to run for the legislature again, and he was going to win. Although he wanted to show up the man who had put the false statement in the newspaper, Crockett really liked representing the people of his Tennessee district.

Once Davy Crockett realized how much his style of campaigning appealed to the voters in his Tennessee district, he became more and more animated and dramatic at each stop, as shown in this undated woodcut.

Campaigning the Crockett Way

Crockett hired a man to take care of his farm, and then set off on the campaign trail. From his observation, Crockett felt the candidate who had the greatest chance of winning—and his greatest competition—was Dr. William E. Butler. Crockett decided to follow the doctor from crowd to crowd. As he had done in past campaigns, Crockett gave his frontier speeches, emphasizing all the things he felt he had in common with the voters. All the while, though, he listened carefully to every word Butler had said. Crockett had a plan that he felt sure would win him the election.

At one of the last gatherings, Crockett asked to speak first, and Butler agreed. Crockett gave Butler's speech word for word! Butler was dumbfounded and had nothing to say when it was his turn to speak. The crowd loved it. Crockett won the election by 247 votes and returned to Murfreesboro in September.

Once again, he championed the rights of the poor people of the state. He also managed to alienate one of the country's most powerful figures—General Andrew Jackson. Crockett felt that Jackson was politically dishonest because he had blocked the reelection of Tennessee Senator John Williams to the U.S. Congress for personal, not political, reasons. In fact, Crockett grew so angry about what Jackson had done that he started to think about running for Congress himself.

Davy Crockett's unwavering support of Andrew Jackson, shown in this Currier & Ives lithograph c. 1845, turned to bitter disappointment once Jackson entered politics.

In 1825, urged on by his supporters, Crockett challenged the **incumbent** congressman, Colonel Adam Alexander. During that era, it was common practice to treat voters to drinks at campaign gatherings in the hopes of winning their votes. Unfortunately for Crockett, the wealthy Alexander could treat voters to as many drinks as they wanted. Crockett, on the other hand, had only his backwoods humor to offer them, and that wasn't enough to make the men vote for him. That August, Crockett lost the election to Congress by 267 votes.

A Disastrous New Business

Now that Crockett was not going to Congress, he had to find a way both to keep busy and to provide an income for his family, so—like the gristmill business—he decided to do something he knew nothing about. He announced that he was going to make wooden **staves** for barrels and ship them south on the Mississippi River for sale in New Orleans.

Crockett figured the first step in his new business was to build a couple of flatboats on which to ship the staves. So he hired some men to do just that on the riverbank by his property—while, of course, he went hunting. Winter was approaching, and Crockett was more concerned about providing enough winter meat for his family than about making the barrel staves

In Colonial America, wooden barrels were used for storing and transporting almost everything. Crockett's new business would make wooden staves for the barrels.

This mid-19th-century painting depicts the type of flatboat Crockett may have built to transport his staves. Unfortunately, his flatboats and their cargo met with a watery end.

himself. That autumn, and on into the next spring, Crockett estimated that he and his hunting companions killed about 107 bears.

When Crockett returned from his hunting trip, the men he had hired had finished the flatboats. They were basically rafts with flat bottoms and square ends. There was also a small room—barely large enough for two people—in the center, to be used for shelter and to store belongings. Oars for rowing and steering were attached to each side.

By February 1826, the men had made almost 30,000 barrel staves. Crockett was pleased with their work, so they set off immediately for New Orleans. When they reached the

Mississippi River, though, Crockett was surprised at how fast the rough currents were carrying the boats along. At that moment, he realized he knew nothing about river navigation. His crew panicked and wanted to abandon the flatboats, but Crockett ordered them to stay put.

In an effort to keep the boats steady, Crockett lashed them together with a length of rope, but that only made them even more unwieldy. There was such bedlam on board that no one could hear the instructions that were being shouted by people on the riverbank who saw what was happening. Unable to reach the safety of shore, Crockett and the two men struggled to keep the boats afloat until they reached calmer waters.

His crew panicked . . . but Crockett ordered them to stay put.

Finally, nearing exhaustion, Crockett went inside the cabin of the lead boat to warm himself on the small fire. Suddenly, pieces of the roof started falling around him. The boat was literally breaking apart. Within minutes, the boats slammed into some submerged trees and started to sink. River water began pouring in, blocking the passageways out of the cabin. Crockett spotted a small hole in the side of the cabin and tried to crawl through, but he was stuck! Luckily, the two men grabbed him and pulled hard to free him, but in the process, they also pulled off Crockett's clothes!

The boats finally went under. Crocket and the men quickly grabbed some floating tree branches and held on until the next morning when a boat sailing north from Memphis rescued them. They were put ashore at a small river town where Crockett "met with a friend, that I never can forget as long as I am able to go ahead at any thing; it was a Major Marcus B. Winchester, a merchant of that place; he [gave us all new clothes], and some little money to go upon, and so we all parted."

Crockett finally made it back home in the spring of 1826 and was now in even greater debt, because of the loss of the boats and the staves. Crockett, though, was true to himself. Rather than worry, he looked forward to hunting more bears and, of all things, to running again for Congress!

Elected to the U.S. Congress

Crockett began his campaign in January of 1827. He had received a generous loan from Major Winchester, the man who had helped him after his Mississippi River accident. Although Crockett again suffered abuses from arrogant candidates, his honesty, humor, and ability to convince voters that he was one of them helped him get elected in August to the U.S. House of Representatives.

Before Crockett headed to Washington, D.C., he decided to take Elizabeth to North Carolina to visit her family. Unfortunately, his malaria flared up again, and he was miserable for most of the trip. As was the custom for the time, the doctor he went to "bled" him by opening his veins and letting the blood run out into pans. At this time, it was believed that in this way the inflected blood would get out of his system. Unfortunately, it only weakened Crockett even more. By the time he finally arrived in Washington and moved into a boarding house near the Capitol Building, he was not in good health. Later, he [wrote], "I have thought that I was never to See my family any more, tho thanks be to god I hope that I am Recovering."

Physicians in the 19th century used the method of "bleeding," as shown in this c. 1804 print, as the best way to cure a patient. Crockett underwent this procedure only to become even more ill.

Nineteenth-Century Medicine

At the beginning of the nineteenth century, doctors believed that all diseases resulted from an excess of fluids in the body and that the way to cure a disease was through bloodletting and **purging**, which would get rid of these fluids. Men such as Benjamin Franklin and Thomas Jefferson had dominated the intellectual life of the United States from 1750 to 1800, and they had promoted scientific research. With such men gone, the knowledge necessary to disprove such beliefs was slow to develop in America.

Nineteenth-century doctors did almost nothing to improve medicine. Even when people began to rebel against painful purging and bloodletting, the doctors were replaced by untrained health reformers who came up with outlandish medical theories of their own. Soon, people were being treated with mostly ineffective remedies such as water, electricity, and vegetable compounds.

For every person in 19th-century America who came up with a crazy "medical remedy"—such as the Common Sense Electric Belt shown in this ad—there was someone even crazier who tried it.

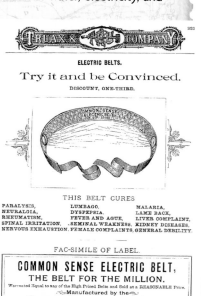

Even though he was not fully recovered, Crockett took his election seriously and did his best to push through a bill that would allow parcels of Tennessee land to be sold to the highest bidders—with the money earmarked for public education. Crockett wanted the price of the land to be low enough that the settlers who already lived on it could afford it. His greatest fear was that the settlers in his western-Tennessee district would lose their land. Unfortunately, Crockett became so ill with repeated bouts of malaria that he missed a number of congressional sessions, and by the time Congress adjourned in May 1828, the land bill had been tabled, or postponed. Crockett was disappointed. That meant nothing could be done about the bill until the next session of Congress.

Another Land Bill Fight

That year, Andrew Jackson defeated John Quincy Adams to become the seventh president of the United States. Crockett returned to Congress in December 1828, and within a few weeks he proposed an amendment to the Tennessee land bill tabled the previous year. He now believed the land should be given to the people who had been living on it. However, the other Tennessee delegation and even President Jackson opposed this idea.

Crockett steadfastly maintained that he only wanted what was best

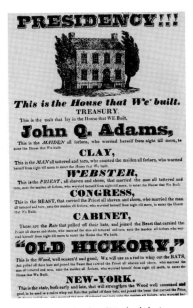

This mean-spirited political ad during the 1828 presidential election praises Andrew Jackson—"Old Hickory"—at the expense of John Quincy Adams, Henry Clay, Daniel Webster, and Congress, among others.

for the people of his district. The other legislators wanted to sell the land to raise money for colleges in the state, but Crockett told them that the children in his district had never seen the inside of a college and probably never would. Once again, he was fighting the elitism of the politicians whom, he was sure, did not really care about poor people.

Nationally, the political parties had begun to **polarize**. The Democrats supported Jackson. The Republicans and the anti-Jackson Democrats became the Whig Party under Henry Clay, a senator from Kentucky. Although Crockett had tried to steer clear of national political brawls, he found himself drawing closer to the Whigs. There were several members of the party staying in the same boarding house where he lived. They defended him in the press from anyone who referred to him as an **uncouth** backwoodsman. They also helped him polish the speeches he gave in front of the Congress.

Crockett continued to push for his version of the Tennessee land bill. When he publicly questioned the motives of the other Tennessee delegates—especially Congressman James K. Polk—for not passing the bill they were all outraged. So committed was Crockett to the passage of his bill, that he began to tell other members of Congress that he would support whatever bills they brought before the house if they would support his. In the end, Crockett wasn't able to get his bill passed, but he was able to delay Polk's version of the bill, and in January 1829, Congress tabled the land bill once again.

The Republicans and the anti-Jackson Democrats formed the Whig Party with Henry Clay of Kentucky as its leader. Davy Crockett found more support among its members than in his own party. Shown here is a portrait of Clay c. 1848.

Whigs v. Democrats

At the start of the twenty-third Congress, which coincided with the second inauguration of Andrew Jackson, the Democratic Republicans had become more generally known simply as Democrats. The party carries the same name today. The National Republicans were more generally known as the Whigs. In Great Britain during the seventeenth century, this term was used by factions opposed to the monarchy. During the nineteenth century, American Whigs saw themselves as a defense against what they considered the excesses of Andrew Jackson. However, the issue of slavery brought an end to the Whig Party. The political fallout from the Compromise of 1850 and the Kansas-Nebraska Act of 1854 caused some Whigs to join the Democratic Party (mostly aligned with Southerners) and others to form a new Republican Party (mostly aligned with Northerners).

This satirical political cartoon of 1850 shows an attempt to balance southern and northern interests on the question of slavery.

Unsavory Political Tactics

When Crockett returned home, he knew he would have a tough campaign ahead of him if he wanted to retain his seat in Congress. He really had little to offer the voters, as he had failed to get the land bill passed. He also learned that the state's other members of Congress, led by Congressman Polk, were going to do everything they could to defeat Crockett.

These other representatives began one of the most negative campaigns in American political history. They told untrue stories about Crockett's being a drunkard and having committed

James K. Polk, shown in this mid-19th-century lithograph, would become the 11th president of the United States, but in 1829, when still a congressman from Tennessee, Davy Crockett was able to delay passage of Polk's version of the land bill.

adultery. They wrote false letters to the newspapers and encouraged the voters to support Polk's version of the land bill and oppose Crockett's. They said, "He associated himself with our political enemies . . . We can't trust him an inch."

For his part, Crockett countered with his own false stories about Polk and the rest of the Tennessee delegation. However, his reasoning and strategy were somewhat different. When Crockett appeared at campaign rallies, he told the crowds that he had been deliberately lying about the other candidates—but he did so because the other candidates had been lying about him. It was a clear case of meeting fire with fire. The crowds understood and loved it.

When the election was finally held in August, Crockett won, winning over Colonel Adam Alexander, the man who had beaten him two years earlier in 1825. It was a special satisfaction to Crockett that even though James K. Polk had also been returned to Congress, the candidate that Polk had chosen to unseat Crockett had been defeated.

Once again, Crockett tried to push through his land bill, but he was still unable to make any progress. Finally, he agreed to a **compromise**, with the land being sold for twelve-and-a-half cents an acre (about $1.50 by today's standards)—a fair price but also a large sum of money for most people—with the settlers having the first right to buy it.

Opposing the President

As Crockett moved closer and closer to the thinking of the Whigs, he became an embarrassment to President Jackson. Crockett did not care. Crockett announced that he would always follow his conscience and would never let any man, even a president, lead him around like a dog on a leash.

The bad blood between Crockett and President Jackson finally came to a head in early 1830 when President Jackson introduced the Indian Removal Bill. It called for uprooting the peaceful southeastern Native Americans and sending them to live on lands west of the Mississippi River. Even though this removal would open more territory for settlers in western Tennessee, Crockett opposed it, not only because Jackson wanted it, but also because he thought it was wrong to move a whole population of people from their

Crockett announced that he would always follow his conscience and would never let any man, even a president, lead him around like a dog on a leash.

ancestral homes. "I believe the measure is unjust and wicked, and I shall fight it, let the consequences be what they may. . . . I would sooner be honest and politically damned than hypocritically immortalized." In May the bill passed, however, and Crockett's vote was the only dissenting one in the Tennessee delegation.

During the summer of 1831, Crockett again faced a tough campaign for reelection. His vote against the Indian Removal Bill had caused him a problem in the eyes of his **constituents**. Now the Tennessee delegation worked even harder to unseat him. They called him not only a traitor to President Jackson, but also a traitor to the entire state of Tennessee.

Crockett tried to fight back, once again using his humor, but he seemed to have lost his easygoing ways. Several times, he threatened to thrash

As Crockett moved closer and closer to the thinking of the Whigs, he became an embarrassment to President Jackson.

his opponents if they made any more accusations against him. When President Jackson told the people in Crockett's district that it would be a disgrace to reelect such a person to represent them, it seemed that was the final straw, and in August Crockett lost the election by more than 500 votes.

Andrew Jackson (1767–1845)

Andrew Jackson first gained fame when he forced the British out of New Orleans in 1815. He was governor of the Florida Territory and a U.S. senator representing Tennessee. In 1824, he was a candidate in the presidential election. When the outcome had to be determined by the House of Representatives, he lost out to John Quincy Adams. Jackson, however, won the election in 1828 and became the seventh president of the United States.

One of Jackson's major accomplishments as president was to make the executive branch as strong as the other two branches of the federal government—the judicial (Supreme Court) and the legislative (the Senate and the Congress). Jackson won reelection in 1832. Because Jackson rewarded many of his political supporters with government jobs while he was president, his critics coined the expression "the spoils system." In 1836, Jackson followed George Washington's example of not running for a third term. After he left Washington, he returned to his native Tennessee. He died in 1845.

No matter how intensely Davy Crockett came to dislike Andrew Jackson in later years, he and other Americans never forgot Jackson's military victories, especially, as depicted here in the Battle of New Orleans during the War of 1812.

CHAPTER 9

Political Disappointments

Since you have chosen to elect a man with a timber toe to succeed me, you may all go to hell and I will go to Texas.

After his election defeat, Crockett returned to Tennessee and spent a lot of time at home reevaluating his life. He consoled himself with the thought that he had been true to his conscience and that he had tried to look out for the poor people of Tennessee. He also farmed and hunted and began borrowing money, not only to pay off some of his debts but also to finance his next campaign for Congress. He still believed that he had a lot of work to do in Washington and a lot of fight left in him. Besides, he enjoyed the status of *congressman*.

The Bank of the United States soon came to his aid. It was originally created in 1791 to handle the financial

Shown in an 1800 print, the Bank of the United States was created in 1791 to handle the financial needs of the federal government. Although Davy Crockett's constituents were opposed to the national bank, Crockett supported it because it helped him financially by paying off his debts.

needs and requirements of the newly formed federal government, and it was still controlled by the Whig Party. When the bank notified Crockett that it was going to pay off his debts, he was extremely grateful.

Crockett Becomes a National Figure

Fortunately for Crockett's upcoming campaign, two things happened which turned him into a national figure. In 1831, a play by James Kirke Paulding titled *The Lion of the West* was produced and featured a character name Nimrod Wildfire— an outlandish but very likeable frontiersman. The play was an enormous success, and everyone who saw it assumed it was based on the life of Davy Crockett. Although Paulding denied the connection, Nimrod Wildfire was forever connected with Crockett.

James Kirke Paulding was the author of the enormously successful play called *The Lion of the West*, which featured a Davy Crockett-like main character.

Two years later, Matthew St. Clair Clarke, the clerk of the U.S. House of Representatives, wrote a book titled *Life and Adventures of Colonel David Crockett of West Tennessee*. It contained many stories that Davy probably shared with Clarke when he was in Washington. Unfortunately, it also included some tales Clarke made up, which exaggerated Crockett's image as an uneducated backwoodsman—something the colonel was trying to change. Like the play, the book was an enormous success, but for Crockett, the fact that other people were making fortunes selling what was purported to be his life story made him angry.

In the spring, Crockett formally launched his congressional campaign. His opponent was the incumbent William Fitzgerald, the man who had defeated him two years earlier. Crockett tried hard to shake his image as an uneducated backwoodsman, but the play and book did not help. On top of these "fictional" works, Andrew Jackson's political friends did everything they could to keep that image alive before the voters. Crockett tried his best to counter the negative impression of being an uneducated frontiersman, and in the end, he won the election in August 1833—but by only 173 votes. Nevertheless, he was going back to Washington, and that was all that mattered to him.

Right away, Crockett began work on the land bill. He introduced a motion to form a committee to determine the best way to dispose of the land in western Tennessee. The motion also required that any written material that dealt with the land bill had to be turned over to the committee. Both of Crockett's proposals passed. It gave him a renewed hope that the land bill might eventually be passed, too.

An early-19th-century engraving shows Davy Crockett trying to convince other members of Congress that his land bill is the best way to dispose of the land in western Tennessee.

A Run for the Presidency?

In 1833, Whig party members from Mississippi approached Crockett and asked if he would become the next Whig presidential candidate. They told him that the party needed someone as popular in the West as Andrew Jackson in order to counter the candidacy of Martin Van Buren, a New Yorker.

The offer was tempting to Crockett. He felt sure that as president of the United States he would be able to give the poor people of Tennessee the land that they wanted. He also saw it as a way to take revenge against the Jacksonian Democrats who had caused him so much grief in his previous campaigns.

With thoughts of becoming the next president, Crockett started to write his autobiography in December 1833. He wanted to create a more positive national image of himself. He received help from Thomas Chilton, a member of the Whigs representing Kentucky, who was also living

Martin Van Buren is shown in this undated portrait. The Whig Party approached Davy Crockett about becoming a presidential candidate in order to counter Van Buren's candidacy.

in the same boarding house. By January 1834, Crockett had already completed 110 pages of what was to be a book of about 200 pages. In addition, he had received letters from interested publishers in New York and Philadelphia who suggested that Crockett go on a national promotional tour once the book was published.

By February, Crockett had signed a contract with Carey and Hart, a publishing house in Philadelphia, and the book was published in March. It was titled *A Narrative of the Life of David*

Davy Crockett's Autobiography

In Crockett's autobiography, *A Narrative of the Life of David Crockett*, he wrote, "As the public seem to feel some interest in the history of an individual so humble as I am, and as that history can be so well known to no person living as to myself, I have, after so long a time, and under many pressing solicitations from my friends and acquaintances, at least determined to put my own hand to it, and lay before the world a narrative on which they may at least rely on being true."

The book is considered one of the most important documents in American history. As a literary work, it is one of the earliest autobiographies, coming just a few years after Benjamin Franklin's, which was the first in a long line of autobiographies written by historical figures. It is also an example of American frontier humor. About trying to talk to a girl, he wrote, "My heart would begin to flutter like a duck in a puddle; and if I tried to outdo it and speak, would get right smack up in my throat, and [choke] me like a cold [potato]." With its use of dialect, expressions, and spellings that represent nonstandard pronunciations, it is an important document in the development of American English. Finally, it is also a valuable historical document of the times.

Davy Crockett's signature as it appeared on signed copies of his autobiography.

Crockett of the State of Tennessee. Except for the publisher's decision to take out some of the references to the brutal attacks on Native Americans during the Creek War, Crockett was satisfied with how the book turned out. He was looking forward to traveling the country and accepting the high praises of the American public.

Crockett's Tour of the Northeast

Davy Crockett's book tour of the Northeast started in the spring of 1834. It was one of the busiest times in Congress, but Crockett wanted to prove to himself and to the rest of the nation that Davy Crockett was a major celebrity and public figure. This was exactly what the Whigs were hoping for—someone who could draw crowds in the East and deliver their anti-Jackson political message. What Crockett didn't realize was that the Whigs considered him politically expendable—meaning they weren't concerned if he damaged his own political reputation—just as long he also damaged President Jackson's.

Everywhere Crockett went, he was wined and dined. He shook thousands of hands and made many anti-Jackson speeches. "Andrew Jackson, both cabinets, and Congress to boot, can't enact poor men into rich." At times, the crowds were so huge that Crockett got stage fright, but someone in the crowd would always bolster his morale by

This profile depicts Davy Crockett at the approximate time of his book tour.

shouting his name and telling him that everyone there was waiting to hear what he had to say. That usually broke the ice for him, and he would launch into his speech. The crowds always cheered. The Whigs loved it, too. Everything was working in their favor.

Soon, though, Crockett sensed that some of the Easterners were coming to see him not for what he had to say but to catch a glimpse of what a "wild man" looked like. He began to feel resentful and ached to be in the woods again with his gun and dogs. Still, he continued the tour and accepted all the gifts that were offered him, including a new rifle that would be made to his specifications and was promised to him by the Young Whigs Organization of Philadelphia.

Crockett's tour took him to major cities in the Northeast. In New York, he saw the awesome sailing ships and remembered how as a boy he had almost gone to sea on one of them. He also visited several newspaper offices at which he hoped to impress the editors so that they would write positive stories about him and negative stories about President Jackson.

While in New Jersey, he participated in a local shooting match—at which he impressed the crowds with his expert marksmanship. When he arrived in Boston, he visited several historical sites relating to the American Revolution. Crockett also visited a school for blind students and was especially impressed by a young blind boy who escorted him around the school. However, Crockett turned down an invitation to visit Harvard University in Cambridge because he knew that honorary degrees were sometimes bestowed on visiting dignitaries. He wanted no part of what he considered an elitist event. Crockett left Boston, touched by the friendliness and generosity of its inhabitants.

In Boston to promote his autobiography, Davy Crockett also visited several historical sites relating to the American Revolution, including the harbor, pictured in this c. 1833 print.

Crockett was so impressed by the ingenuity and industry of New Englanders that he planned to share his experiences with his own constituents and to bring the message that working hard and saving money was what being an American was all about. That message also impressed the Whigs.

On the morning of May 11, Crockett took a steamboat back to Baltimore and then a stagecoach to Washington. Although he was very tired by the tour, he knew he was going to miss all of the attention he had received. He also admitted to himself that he honestly was not looking forward to returning to Congress. Even so, the Whigs were delighted with Crockett's trip, as he had been very successful at promoting their anti-Jackson message.

Back in Congress

Although Crockett had been buoyed by the attention of the crowds during his trip East and by the support of the Whigs, he still had very little success getting his bills through Congress. That frustrated him so much that he began attacking President Jackson and his supporters even harder. Instead of getting his message across, though, he was fast becoming a bothersome figure not only to Jackson's supporters but also to the rest of the legislators. On June 17, Crockett ranted against Jackson's advisors, "[They] are as hungry as the flies . . . in Aesop's Fables, that came after the fox and sucked his blood. . . . [T]hey are a hungry swarm, and will lick up every dollar of public money."

Instead of getting his message across, though, he was fast becoming a bothersome figure . . .

Soon, Crockett started skipping sessions. Sometimes, in the middle of a debate, he would leave the capitol building and meet with John Gadsby Chapman, an artist who would paint some of the last images of him. They became good friends, and Crockett felt he could tell Chapman anything that was on his mind. At first, Chapman's sketches of him didn't appeal to Crockett, who felt they didn't capture the frontier spirit. After a few suggestions from Crockett, though, Chapman was able to convey the image that the frontiersman had of himself. He dressed Crockett in a hunting shirt, leggings, and moccasins and with a butcher knife and hatchet. He also surrounded him with "hunting dogs," which turned out to be mongrels taken from the streets of Washington, D.C. Chapman was able to capture the right pose when Crockett entered his studio one morning and let out a blood-curdling yell from his frontier days. Upon completion of the portrait, Crockett was most pleased.

Davy Crockett's favorite full portrait of himself was painted by John Gadsby Chapman. He felt it captured the spirit of the American frontier.

Crockett Leaves Washington Early

In 1834, Congress decided to extend its adjournment date until June 30, so there would be more time to pass some last-minute bills. Crockett was disappointed because he had had enough of politics and wanted to leave. Finally, he could no longer stand being in Washington. A few days before the end of the extension, he departed for Philadelphia, where the Young Whigs gave him the rifle they had promised, along with a tomahawk and a hunting knife.

Crockett finally arrived at Mill's Point, Tennessee, on July 22. His son William met him, and they rode home together. For the rest of the summer, Crockett struggled with his ongoing financial problems. Then, in early fall, his father came to live with him but died shortly after arriving.

Crockett was also burdened by Democratic accusations that he was absent from Congress more than he was present. Crockett countered that he had been ill and needed to travel for his health. No one really believed him, but that did not seem to concern Crockett. His reelection campaign wouldn't begin until the following summer, and by then, he was sure, people would have forgotten all about his absences. Deep down, Crockett knew he liked the *idea* of being a congressman more than he actually liked being one and doing the job.

Deep down, Crockett knew he liked the idea of being a congressman more than he actually liked being one . . .

Before Congress reconvened in December 1834, Crockett arranged with William Clark, a Whig representative from Pennsylvania, to put the details of his northeastern tour in a book. Once again, he entered into a contract with the publishers Carey and Hart.

Back in Washington, Crockett again tried to pass bills that would help the people in the western part of Tennessee, but he was not successful this time either. He was now known for having no positive results in his entire congressional career. Even the Whigs started backing away from him.

The End of a Political Career

It is hard to imagine that Crockett ever seriously entertained the notion that he would one day be president of the United States, but when Martin Van Buren received President Jackson's personal endorsement, Crockett knew he would never have a chance, especially now that the Whig Party was also trying to distance itself from him.

Ever since 1827, with his first election to Congress, Crockett had fought to make the land in western Tennessee available and affordable for the people who had settled it. He spent his last days in Congress continuing his fight, again, to no avail. He delivered his last speech on February 20, 1835. When Crockett returned to Tennessee, though, he still had every intention of going back to Washington and resuming the battle.

In March 1835, his book *An Account of Col. Crockett's Tour to the North and Down East in the Year of Our Lord One Thousand Eight Hundred and Thirty Four* was published and became an immediate success. Although it gave a boost to Crockett's political campaign for Congress, Crockett had lost the confidence of the voters, and his opponent Adam Huntsman beat him by 252 votes.

A political cartoon from the 1836 presidential campaign depicts the various candidates as horses and jockeys competing in a horse race.

Although Crockett didn't admit it, his defeat may have come as a relief, because for some time he had been thinking about moving his family farther west, to Texas—a vast new territory that was still a part of northern Mexico.

This map of eastern Texas was drawn by Stephen Austin in 1822 and shows the vastness of the territory, something that appealed to Davy Crockett, who was always looking for a "better" place to live. The green area likely represents the huge amounts of pine forests in that area.

CHAPTER 10

Off to Texas

[I would] rather be a member of the [Texas Constitutional] Convention than of the Senate of the United States.

Because the state of Tennessee was becoming more and more crowded, Davy Crockett made up his mind to move to Texas even though there was rising tension in the territory between the American settlers and the Mexican government. After being part of Mexico's larger state of *Coahuila y Téjas* (Coahuila and Texas), this vast new territory was now seeking independence from Mexico, which was now led by General Antonio López de Santa Anna—president and head of its military.

Print of General Antonio López de Santa Anna c. 1847, the arrogant, cruel, and temperamental ruler of Mexico.

Leaving Tennessee

On November 1, 1835, Crockett set out for Texas. He was accompanied by two of his neighbors, Lindsay K. Tinkle and Abner Burgin, and his nephew, William Patton. He never once looked back. Leaving Tennessee now seemed to him the most natural thing to do. He was attracted not only by the enormous amount of land available to settlers but also at the thought of being involved

The New Republic of Texas

In 1713, the French, having lost their territories in Canada, established a foothold in Louisiana. The government of the Spanish-held territories in North America, fearing further French settlement, claimed Texas, the immense territory to the west, in 1716. At that time, Texas was a remote outpost, sparsely settled. Most of the land was still under the control of Native Americans—the Apaches and the Comanches—and contact with the Spanish government in Mexico City was poor.

A modern-day mural depicts Sam Houston as president of the Texas Republic, entering the new city of Houston in 1837.

When France sold the Louisiana Territory to the United States in 1803, Americans started crossing the Louisiana border into Texas in search of new land to settle. By 1821, the year Mexico received its independence from Spain, Texas was already home to thousands of settlers from the United States. In 1824, Texas was merged with the Mexican state of *Coahuila*.

Then, in 1835, Texas declared its independence from Mexico to become the Republic of Texas. At the time, Texas was smaller than it is today and covered only forty percent of the modern state. Davy Crockett joined other Texans in their fight for independence.

in battles with the Mexican government "and [to] give the [Texans] a helping hand on the high road to freedom."

Crockett and the other men arrived in Memphis, Tennessee, on November 10 and stayed there for a few days, drinking with friends and enjoying themselves. When Crockett and his party finally boarded a ferry to cross the Mississippi into Arkansas, he had no idea he was leaving Tennessee for the last time. They arrived in Little Rock on the evening of November 12 and went straight to the Charles Jeffries City Hotel.

When local officials learned that the famous Davy Crockett was in town, they organized a dinner for him, which he happily accepted. After the meal, he gave the obligatory anti-Jackson speech but now added his "off to Texas" comments to it and boasted that he would "have Santa Anna's head, and wear it for a watch seal [the cover of a pocket watch]." The next morning, Crockett and the three men headed southwest, where they crossed the Red River into Texas.

Texas, a New Frontier

Crockett was enthralled by what he saw. Texas seemed to offer everything he was looking for. There was plenty of land, and there was plenty of game. In fact, Crockett and his companions disappeared for several days to hunt and did not tell anyone in the area where they were going. The local residents were sure they had either been taken hostage or killed by Indians. Their deaths were even reported in some of the newspapers on the East Coast.

On January 8, Crockett and his men arrived in San Augustine, Texas, just west of the Sabine River. Crockett told the crowds that greeted them that he would "rather be a member of the [Texas Constitutional] Convention than of the Senate of the United

Davy Crockett thought he and his family could start a new life in the Texas pine forests that bordered the Red River.

States." While there, Crockett also sent a letter home telling his family that Texas was the garden spot of the world because of the pine forests and the lakes. He added that he was thinking about settling on almost 5,000 acres of land on the Red River.

From San Augustine, Crockett and his men headed to Nacogdoches, where on January 12, 1836, Crockett and his nephew enlisted in the Texas Army. Crockett had two reasons for doing this: He saw it as the fastest way to get the land he wanted—because the Texas government was giving a reward of land to all men who served. He decided this would also put him in a position to help write the Texas constitution when the new republic was finally free from Mexico. The two other men, Burgin and Tinkle, did not enlist and shortly afterward returned to Tennessee.

At the request of his superior officers, Crockett formed a small group of the enlistees into a mounted scout company—very much like the one he had ridden with during the Creek War. Within days, the company headed into the interior of Texas, ready to fight the Mexican army.

Arriving in San Antonio

Crockett and his men arrived in the town of San Antonio sometime during the first week of February. Several months before, a small group of Texans had attacked San Antonio and had forced Mexican troops to take refuge in a small **mission** known as the Alamo on the other side of the San Antonio River. On December 9, the Mexicans finally surrendered but were released.

This 1861 illustration shows the Alamo after a group of Texans forced the Mexican soldiers inside to surrender on December 9, 1835. This event eventually led to General Santa Anna's attack on the Alamo three months later.

San Antonio was now under the command of Lieutenant Colonel James Clinton Neill. Because both the fledgling government and the Texas Army were disorganized, the numbers in his force dwindled slowly as the men, bored with inactivity, left to take care of their families. This constant loss of men only added to the disorder. In early January, Neill had sent out a request for more military support. He knew that Mexico would send its army to reclaim San Antonio, the most important city in the territory, and when it did, it would easily defeat his small force.

It's quite possible that Crockett and his company went to San Antonio because of Neill's request—or they could have simply decided to go there on their own. Nevertheless, even before Crockett reached San Antonio, other reinforcements had arrived, most notably a volunteer force led by Louisianan James Bowie and a small company of regular cavalry under the command of William Barret Travis, a lawyer from South Carolina.

Shortly after Crockett's arrival, a scout returned to San Antonio and reported that the Mexican army, under the command of Santa Anna, had just crossed the Rio Grande. Together, Crockett,

James Bowie, one of the heroes of the Alamo battle, was also famous for the long fighting knife that carried his name.

Travis, and Bowie decided that it would take the Mexican troops at least two weeks to reach San Antonio.

An Army of Volunteers

In the next few days, several problems almost brought an end to the notion that the Texans could make a stand against the Mexicans. The volunteers were leaving the city in droves, and even Neill was called away because of an illness in his family. When he appointed Travis as commander of San Antonio, Neill created another problem.

Volunteers were used to electing their own officers, and they didn't want Travis. They wanted Jim Bowie. Travis agreed to their demands, and Jim Bowie immediately took over, not only the garrison but the town as well and tried to stop everyone from leaving.

This 20th-century drawing by Norman Price depicts William B. Travis with his troops. He told them at the Alamo that they may escape now or cross the line and die with him fighting the Mexican Army.

When Bowie decided to release prisoners, both military and civilian, for work details, Travis, who didn't want criminals having any role in the coming battle, tried to intercede and to regain some control of the situation. Finally, Colonel Neill returned, and he split the command between Bowie and Travis: Travis would command the regular troops and the cavalry. Bowie would command the volunteers.

Crockett, who was quite familiar with problems that arose when volunteers elected their officers, tried to stay out of the argument. "I have come to assist Travis as a high Private," he said. From all accounts, he succeeded. With the garrison's leadership controversy over, there was little they could all do but hope that the additional reinforcements that Colonel Neill had requested would arrive before the Mexican army did.

> *Crockett, who was quite familiar with problems that arose when volunteers elected officers, tried to stay out of the arguement.*

CHAPTER 11

Remember the Alamo!

I am besieged, by a thousand or more of the Mexicans under Santa Anna.

—William Barret Travis

The first soldiers of the Mexican army, with Santa Anna leading them, arrived on the outskirts of San Antonio on the afternoon of February 23, 1836. Santa Anna had hoped to catch the Texans unaware. Fortunately, both Travis and Bowie saw the army approaching and quickly abandoned the town itself and moved all of their men just across the east side of the San Antonio River to the Alamo, a former Catholic mission that had been turned into a military stronghold.

By 3:30 p.m., the Mexican army had taken possession of the town, encountering almost no resistance, and had encircled the Alamo.

An Untimely Cannon Firing

When Santa Anna raised a red flag, a signal to the Alamo defenders that he would take no prisoners, the Texans responded by firing a cannon at him. Within minutes after the shot, one of the Texans reported that Santa Anna had sent one of his soldiers with the message that the general wanted to talk to the Texans. If the message had been received before the cannon was fired, it might have resulted in a compromise and possibly the Battle of the Alamo would never have taken place.

When Bowie learned of Santa Anna's desire to meet, he sent Green Jameson, one of the engineers, with a white flag of truce. However, it was too late; the cannon had already been fired and Santa Anna had changed his mind. The Mexican general rebuffed Jameson and told him that he would not under any circumstances come to terms with such rebellious foreigners. He further added that if they wished to save their lives they should surrender immediately.

After Jameson returned, Travis decided to send his own messenger to Santa Anna's top aide—Colonel Juan Nepomuceno Almonte—to ask him for a meeting. Travis considered Nepomuceno a highly educated person. He knew that the colonel had spent a lot of time visiting the United States, but Travis's man was also rebuffed. Nepomuceno told him that he could not make such decisions for the Mexican government.

Colonel Juan Nepomuceno Almonte was Santa Anna's top aide. He was unable to dissuade the general from attacking the Alamo.

Inside the Alamo

At this time, there were only 150 men inside the Alamo to defend it. They knew they were outnumbered by the Mexicans, ten to one. Some civilian residents of San Antonio had also taken refuge inside the mission just before Santa Anna's first troops had arrived. The group included wives and children and other relatives of the defenders, as well as a few slaves who belonged to some of the men. These people were not expected to join the battle.

They knew they were outnumbered by the Mexicans, ten to one.

Jim Bowie had suddenly become ill and was in no condition to fight, so he was taken to a room just off the barracks. He told his sister-in-law, Juana Alsbury, "Sister, do not be afraid. I leave you with Col. Travis, Col. Crockett, and other friends. They are gentlemen, and will treat you kindly." Now it was left to Travis to take over the command. Crockett held no official position, other than command over his small company of men, but he offered to help Travis in any way he could.

Luckily, before the arrival of the Mexican troops, a small herd of cattle had been driven into the mission. In addition, almost one hundred bushels of corn had earlier been taken from nearby vacant houses. No one would go hungry for a while. There was also water available from an irrigation ditch that flowed through the grounds, but Travis decided that wells should be dug just in case Santa Anna stopped the flow of water in the ditch.

This undated lithograph shows the Mexican army laying siege to the Alamo.

Outside the Alamo, Santa Anna's men set up cannons at strategic places around the mission in an attempt to cut off access to and from the fort. Nevertheless, Travis did manage to send out messengers on horses to spread the news of their plight in a letter to "the People of Texas and All Americans in the World."

Travis's Famous Letter from the Alamo

During Santa Anna's siege of the Alamo, William B. Travis wrote a letter on February 24, 1836, which he addressed "To the People of Texas and All Americans in the World." It read in part:

"I am besieged, by a thousand or more of the Mexicans under Santa Anna. I have sustained a continual Bombardment & cannonade for 24 hours & have not lost a man. . . . I shall never surrender or retreat. . . . I call on you in the name of Liberty, of patriotism & everything dear to the American character, to come to our aid. . . . If this call is neglected, I am determined to . . . die like a soldier who never forgets what is due to his own honor & that of his country. Victory or Death."

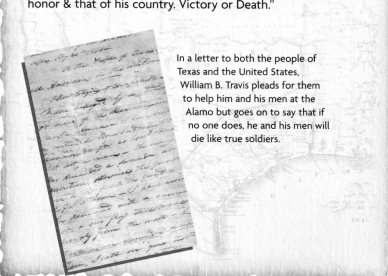

In a letter to both the people of Texas and the United States, William B. Travis pleads for them to help him and his men at the Alamo but goes on to say that if no one does, he and his men will die like true soldiers.

The First Attack

On February 25, Santa Anna sent almost three hundred of his troops to attack the Alamo. He wanted to see how easy or how difficult it would be to breach the walls. The Mexicans were unprepared for the fighting ability and the bravery of the Texans. Two of the Alamo defenders even left the compound during the battle in order to set fire to some buildings that had been providing cover for Santa Anna's troops.

According to Travis, the defenders, including Davy Crockett, showed extreme courage and bravery during the battle. Travis

In this lithograph, the defenders of the Alamo show extreme courage and bravery against overwhelming odds.

wrote, "You have no doubt seen my official report of the action of the 25th [of last month] in which we repulsed the enemy with considerable loss; on the night of the 25th they made another attempt to charge us in the rear of the fort, but we received them gallantly by a discharge of grape shot and [musket fire], and they took to their [outlying buildings for cover]."

Although this first attack was repulsed from inside the Alamo, the defenders could easily see Santa Anna's army increase in strength almost hourly. It seemed to them as if there were an unbroken line of Mexican troops all the way to Mexico City!

While Travis was officially in command of the Alamo, he very much depended on Crockett's judgment and advice on what should be done next in the battle. To the men inside, Davy Crockett was a national hero. He was considered more of a natural leader than Travis, although Crockett made sure he never disobeyed Travis's orders and always treated him as his superior.

No Major Reinforcements

Thirty-two Texas soldiers from Gonzales slipped through the lines of Santa Anna's troops and into the Alamo on March 1. Travis was happy to have the reinforcements, but he knew more were desperately needed.

On March 2, representatives of the Texas government met in Washington-on-the-Brazos and

Thousands of Mexican soldiers begin their final assault on the Alamo.

declared themselves independent from Mexico. They hoped that what was happening at the Alamo would be the first victory against Mexico as an independent country. By then, Santa Anna had been bombarding the Alamo with cannons for eight days. His men were entrenched on all sides of the mission. Still, inside, the spirits were high, kept that way in part by the positive attitude of Davy Crockett, who continuously extolled his faith in volunteer soldiers.

Although Travis still had received only meager reinforcements, he did get some encouraging news on March 3 from messengers who had been able to slip through Santa Anna's troops. Some men from Goliad, under the command of Colonel James W. Fannin, were on their way, along with several pieces of artillery. He was told, "For God's sake hold out until we can assist you." Unfortunately, almost at the same time, the rest of Santa Anna's army finally showed up. He now had enough troops to storm the Alamo.

Travis considered James W. Fannin, pictured here, his last hope. But for numerous reasons, Colonel Fannin was unable to get his troops to the Alamo in time to battle the Mexicans.

On March 3, under the cover of darkness, Travis sent Crockett and two other men to find Fannin and his men. At the time, they didn't know that Fannin had decided to give up going to the Alamo. He used the excuse that several of the wagons were broken. Fortunately, Crockett's group encountered about fifty men from a number of small units who were also trying to reach the Alamo. Crockett and one of the other men led the volunteers back to the mission. Crockett sent the other man on to Gonzales to see what the delay was.

When no reinforcements appeared by the next day, Travis penned an angry and bitter letter to a friend in which he declared that he would defend the Alamo with or without the help of the rest of the citizens of Texas who he felt neglected their duty. "I think we had better march out and die in the open air. I don't like to be hemmed up," Travis privately told Susanna Dickenson, one of the women who had taken refuge inside the Alamo.

Santa Anna Attacks

On March 5, the twelfth day of the siege, Santa Anna announced that his assault on the Alamo would begin the next day. His officers were stunned at the order. After all, the walls of the Alamo were crumbling, no Texas relief columns were expected, and when the Texans ran out of food, they would only have one option left: surrender. Santa Anna refused to listen to his officers' arguments.

Right before dawn on Sunday morning, March 6, 1836, a bugle sounded, and Santa Anna ordered 1,800 of his soldiers to attack the Alamo. They pressed forward with the rat-tat-tat of drums and exploding cannon shells. The Texas defenders, using their few cannons and rifles, forced the Mexicans to retreat and regroup. When the Mexicans attacked the

Having breached the walls of the compound, the Mexican troops stormed the chapel and the adjoining buildings of the Alamo.

Amid the dead and the dying, the Texans, with their backs to the wall, fire at the approaching Mexican troops in this c. 1912 print.

Alamo the second time, they got past the outer wall. Many of the Texans, including Travis, were quickly cut down by the overwhelming number of Mexican soldiers.

The remaining Texans withdrew to the sanctuary and to rooms in the long barracks (formerly the convent), but the Mexicans fought their way into the church in blazes of burning gunpowder and clouds of smoke. They used battering rams to break through walls and doors. When their ammunition gave out, the Texans fought the Mexicans with their bare hands, but they were no match for the bullets and bayonets of Santa Anna's soldiers. Jim Bowie, still too ill to get out of bed, died there. Although Crockett's nephew, William Patton, was never actually listed among the dead, historians believe it was just an oversight and that he in fact died during the fighting. The entire battle took no more than ninety minutes.

It is believed that as many as seven of the defenders remained alive, Crockett among them, although this is still debated by historians. According to surviving papers of some of the combatants on both sides, the men were taken to Santa Anna who ordered them executed immediately. The surviving women, children, and slaves were allowed to leave the mission unharmed.

Santa Anna ordered his men to take the bodies of the Texans to a nearby stand of trees where they were stacked together and wood piled on top of them. That evening, a fire was lit, and the defenders of the Alamo were burned to ashes.

Their ammunition almost exhausted, the few remaining Texans fight in hand-to-hand combat as the Mexican soldiers make their way into the barracks.

Antonio López de Santa Anna (1794–1876)

Santa Anna began his long military career as a cadet at the age of sixteen. In 1833, he became president of Mexico, but he soon tired of the office and let his vice president handle the day-to-day business. When the vice president angered some powerful people in the country, Santa Anna retook power. He sowed the seeds of the Texas Revolution when he rewrote Mexico's 1824 constitution so he would have more power.

American settlers and many Mexicans living in Texas realized that they had nothing to gain by remaining part of Mexico. When the revolution finally came in 1835, Santa Anna himself led a "take-no-prisoners" attack on the Alamo in San Antonio. He was defeated by Sam Houston at the Battle of San Jacinto a few weeks later. Santa Anna was eventually allowed to return to Mexico where he reestablished his power and authority in 1836. In 1846, Mexico suffered a crushing defeat in a war with the United States, but Santa Anna still remained one of the most powerful figures in Mexico. In 1853, he was deposed after he sold millions of acres of land in what is now southern Arizona and New Mexico to the United States. He never again returned to political power and died in 1876.

Even after his defeat a few weeks later by Sam Houston at the Battle of San Jacinto, Santa Anna remained in power in Mexico until 1853. In this undated engraving, he is shown with his assistant, Arista, in 1843.

CHAPTER 12

The Death of a Man/ The Birth of a Legend

"He was indeed a character, one that no other country but our own ever did or ever will produce."

——New York Sunday Morning News, May 1, 1836

After the fall of the Alamo, the Mexican army headed east, easily pushing back Texan troops. When Santa Anna's troops reached the San Jacinto River; however, there was a stalemate, and both sides used the time to regroup. Fortunately for the Texans, the Mexicans became **complacent**. On April 21, Sam Houston and his forces attacked the Mexican camp. In fewer than twenty minutes, the Texans had either killed or captured every Mexican soldier. Santa Anna was now a prisoner. For all intents and purposes, even though there were still Mexican troops on Texas soil, the revolution had ended. Texas would soon become an independent republic.

Following the Battle of San Jacinto on April 21, 1836, Santa Anna surrendered to General Sam Houston, which is depicted in this engraving.

Sam Houston (1793–1863)

Sam Houston was a leader of Texas independence, the first president of the Republic of Texas, and the namesake of the city of Houston. After the death of his father in 1807, his family moved to Tennessee. In 1809, Houston ran away from home to live with the Cherokee. He was adopted into the Cherokee nation and given the name *Colloneh*, "the raven." He returned home in 1812 and enlisted in the army to fight the British. During the war, he became a friend of Andrew Jackson, and later he was a Tennessee congressman.

Sam Houston, shown here in a photograph taken between 1848 and 1850, was a major figure in Texas history.

Houston was also governor of Tennessee, but less than a year into his term he suddenly resigned and went to live again among the Cherokee. He moved to Texas in 1832. When Texas declared its independence from Mexico in 1836, Houston became a Major General in the Texas Army. After the Battle of the Alamo that same year, Houston's troops defeated General Santa Anna at the Battle of San Jacinto. Houston became an instant hero.

When Texas joined the United States in 1845, Houston went to Congress as one of its senators and served three terms. In 1859, he was elected governor of the state of Texas. When the Civil War began, Texas seceded from the Union, but Houston refused to pledge allegiance to the Confederate States of America and was forced out as governor. Two years later, he died in Huntsville, Texas.

News of Crockett's Death

It wasn't long before news of the fall of the Alamo spread eastward, finally reaching Crockett's family, who were devastated by what they heard. However, his daughter Matilda said that the family was holding out hope that he was still alive. Because they had several times before received rumors of her father's death only to have him reappear, she felt he would soon be walking down the road toward them, dressed in his buckskins, his Kentucky Long Rifle slung over his shoulder, and grinning from ear to ear.

It lifted their spirits and increased their hopes even more when newspapers such as *The Morning Courier* and *New York Enquirer* began printing reports that Crockett was "still alive and grinning." Where all of these stories came from is hard to say, but they turned out to be untrue, and Crockett's family and America began a slow adjustment to his death.

It wasn't long before news of the fall of the Alamo spread eastward, finally reaching Crockett's family . . .

After Crockett died fighting at the Alamo, he became an even more popular figure in American history, and by 1845, when journalist John L. O'Sullivan coined the phrase "Manifest Destiny"—the belief that the United States was destined to expand from the Atlantic coast to the Pacific coast—Davy Crockett's life and growing legend seemed to personify that concept.

When Richard Penn Smith's exaggerated *Col. Crockett's Exploits and Adventures in Texas* appeared shortly after Crockett's death, Crockett's place in the popular culture of the United States was firmly established. Americans couldn't get enough of stories about him. *Davy Crockett's Almanack* was first published in 1835,

In this c. 1873 lithograph a woman representing "Manifest Destiny" leads American settlers west.

but after 1836, these magazines started including more and more outrageous stories. In them, Crockett was doing everything from taming wild animals and riding up Niagara Falls on an alligator to battling comets.

Once again, in 1840, stories began to surface that Davy Crockett was still alive. William C. White, an American who had been living in Mexico, said he had spoken to a prisoner working in a mine near the city of Guadalajara who said he was Crockett. The man asked White to take a letter to Crockett's family in Tennessee.

The *Austin Gazette* published an article detailing White's meeting with the prisoner, but it didn't publish the contents of the letter. White said he had sent the original letter to Tennessee via Matamoros, Mexico, and New Orleans, but the letter never reached the Crockett family. Although White said he had made a copy of the letter, he never revealed its details.

John Wesley Crockett, now a member of Congress, decided to follow up on White's information. John Wesley had never been fully convinced that his father had actually died at the Alamo, even though he was aware that there were survivors of the Alamo who had identified his father's body.

After his death, Davy Crockett's memory was kept alive by the fantastic stories about him that appeared in *Davy Crockett's Almanack.*

In addition, he had also heard another story that told of how Santa Anna, as a prisoner, had reported that even after Colonel Almonte had asked him to spare Davy's life, the general still ordered Crockett to be killed. Aware of Almonte's background, John Wesley hoped that perhaps Almonte had disobeyed Santa Anna's orders and had secretly taken his father out of Texas.

John Wesley wrote to Secretary of State John Forsyth asking that his father's death be investigated. Although Forsyth did as John Wesley had requested, the information he finally received was not what he was hoping for. According to the American minister to Mexico, the only information he was able to uncover was that the prisoner White talked to had died. For the Crockett family, that news ended all hope that Davy Crockett was still alive.

Davy Crockett Still Lives On

After the American Civil War, a new generation learned about Davy through the play *Davy Crockett; or, Be Sure You're Right, Then Go Ahead*, which debuted in 1872 and ran until 1896.

In 1909, a silent film titled *Davy Crockett—in Hearts United* ran in movie houses to packed audiences. Other films, books, and magazine articles continued to appear, all appealing to Americans who couldn't seem to get enough of Davy Crockett.

The 1950s was the most celebrated decade for Davy Crockett. This was when Walt Disney produced a three-part television series called *Davy Crockett, King of the Wild Frontier*. It created an unprecedented merchandising craze for almost anything with Crockett's image on it.

Actor Fess Parker played Davy Crockett in the television series produced by Walt Disney. For many Americans during the 1950s, Parker made the spririt of Davy Crockett come alive.

The Marketing of Davy Crockett

Walt Disney understood how popular culture could manipulate historical figures, so he took the legend of Davy Crockett and remade it to fit television audiences of the 1950s. The series became the biggest overnight hit in television history. It arrived just about the same time that television sets were beginning to appear in most homes, bringing about a major change in American society.

Mass-market advertisers soon discovered that parents would buy almost anything associated with Davy Crockett. Their children especially wanted a coonskin cap, just like Davy's (Disney version), so they could hunt "b'ars" in their backyards. As a result, raccoon skin prices jumped dramatically. Because Disney was unable to copyright the Crockett name, hundreds of products quickly appeared on the market, including guitars, underwear, moccasins, bedspreads, lunch boxes, books, comics, and toothbrushes. In order not to be left out of this craze, some companies simply pasted Crockett labels on whatever western-type merchandise they had. It worked.

American children could not get enough of Davy Crockett. They read books about him and wore coonskin hats along with Davy Crockett shirts and jeans. They also carried Davy Crockett lunch boxes to school.

In the end, we may never know where truth stops and legend begins, but it almost doesn't matter, because Davy Crockett the man and Davy Crockett the legend clearly defended the same values. They both epitomized the American spirit of exploring the unsettled lands of a young country, and they both struggled for the common people, defining for their time just what it meant to be an American. Besides, in the view of many Americans, "when no one sees a legend die, then the legend lives."

This statue of Davy Crockett stands in the Texas State History Museum.

Glossary

appealed—asked that a higher court reconsider a ruling.

bill—proposal for a new law.

complacent—to be so smug as to let one's guard down.

compromise—settlement of differences in which each person or party gives up something.

constituents—residents of a politician's district.

drovers—people who herd (drive) sheep or cattle to market.

electors—qualified voters in an election.

hammocks—devices made out of canvas strips or netting that are hung between two poles and used for sleeping.

homesteader—a person who acquires a tract of land from the government by filing a claim and then living on and cultivating the land.

imperial system—relating to standards in Great Britain.

incumbent—the current holder of a political office.

indentured—bound by contract to work for another person for a certain number of years.

legal tender—anything that can be offered in payment for goods or services.

legislator—a person who creates or enacts laws.

literate—able to read and write.

militia—a citizen army as distinct from a professional army.

mission—a Catholic church with no priest of its own.

parasites—microscopic organisms that attach themselves to an organ of the body and feed off it.

polarize—to break into opposing groups.

purging—process of getting rid of something unwanted.

spleen—human organ concerned with the filtration and storage of blood.

staves—narrow strips of wood used to make barrels.

stockade—a barrier made of strong posts or timber driven into the ground and used for protection from attacks.

tyranny—the cruel use of power.

uncouth—behaving crudely.

volleys—the back and forth firings of weapons by opposing forces.

wagoners—people who transported goods by wagons.

wampum—beads of polished shells strung together and used by American Indians as money.

warrants—authorizations for actions such as search, seizure, or arrest.

Bibliography

Burke, James Wakefield. *Davy Crockett, the Man behind the Myth*. Austin, Texas: Eakin Press, 1984.

Cobia, Manley F., Jr. *Journey into the Land of Trials: The Story of Davy Crockett's Expedition to the Alamo*. Franklin, Tennessee: Hillsboro Press, 2003.

Crockett, David. *Davy Crockett, His Own Story: A Narrative of the Life of David Crockett of the State of Tennessee*. Bedford, Massachusetts: Applewood Books, 1993.

———. *Davy Crockett, His Own Story: A Narrative of the Life of David Crockett of the State of Tennessee*. Facsimile edition. Knoxville: University of Tennessee Press, 1973.

Davis, William C. *Three Roads to the Alamo: The Lives and Fortunes of David Crockett, James Bowie, and William Barret Travis*. New York: HarperCollins Publishers, 1998.

Derr, Mark. *The Frontiersman: The Real Life and the Many Legends of Davy Crockett*. New York: William Morrow, 1993.

Groneman III, William. *David Crockett, Hero of the Common Man*. New York: Forge, 2005.

Holbrook, Stewart H. *Davy Crockett*. New York: Random House, 1955.

Hollmann, Robert. *Davy Crockett*. Dallas: Durban House Publishing Company, 2005.

Jones, Randell. *In the Footsteps of Davy Crockett*. Winston-Salem, North Carolina: John F. Blair, Publisher, 2006.

Kilgore, Dan. *How Did Davy Die?* College Station and London: Texas A&M University Press, 1978.

Lofaro, Michael, ed. *Davy Crockett: The Man, the Legend, the Legacy, 1786–1986*. Knoxville: University of Tennessee Press, 1985.

———. and Joe Cummings, eds. *Crockett at Two Hundred: New Perspectives on the Man and the Myth*. Knoxville: University of Tennessee Press, 1989.

Rourke, Constance. *Davy Crockett*. New York: Harcourt, Brace and Co., 1934. Reprint, illustrated by James MacDonald; introduction to the Bison Books edition by Michael A. Lofaro. Lincoln, Nebraska: University of Nebraska Press, 1998.

Sanford, William R. and Carl R. Green. *Davy Crockett, Defender of the Alamo*. Berkeley Heights, New Jersey: Enslow Publisher, Inc., 1996.

Shackford, James A. *David Crockett: The Man and the Legend*. Chapel Hill, North Carolina: University of North Carolina Press, 1956.

Source Notes

The following list contains citations for the sources of the quoted material found in this book. The first and last few words of each quotation are cited and followed by its source. Complete information on referenced sources can be found in the Bibliography.

Abbreviations used:

DCMM—*Davy Crockett, the Man behind the Myth*

JLT—*Journey into the Land of Trials: The Story of Davy Crockett's Expedition to the Alamo*

TRA—*Three Roads to the Alamo: The Lives and Fortunes of David Crockett, James Bowie, and William Barret Travis*

TF—*The Frontiersman: The Real Life and Many Legends of Davy Crockett*

DCHCM—*Davy Crockett, Hero of the Common Man*

DC—*Davy Crockett*

DCML—*David Crockett: The Man and the Legend*

DCHOS—*Davy Crockett, His Own Story*

NYSMN—*New York Sunday Morning News, May 1, 1836*

INTRODUCTION: The Legend of Davy Crockett
   PAGE 1 *"Burn Crockett . . . rebels."*: DCMM, p. 274

Chapter 1: Child of the Frontier
   PAGE 2 *"There must . . . to myself."*: DCHCM, p. 109
   PAGE 7 *"[Davy is] not . . . and learns."*: DCMM, p. 14
   PAGE 8 *"I got the . . . satisfied."*: TRA, p. 16
   PAGE 9-10 *"I scratched . . . for [mercy]."*: TF, p. 46
   PAGE 11 *"[He had been] . . . the fur fly."*: DCHCM, p. 28

Chapter 2: A Difficult Journey Home
   PAGE 12 *"I often . . . he carried."*: TRA, p. 19
   PAGE 12 *"I often . . . he carried."*: TRA, p. 19
   PAGE 17 *"A mighty . . . tell you."*: DCHCM, p. 33
   PAGE 19 *"shed . . . tears."*: TF, p. 50

Chapter 3: Courtin' and Marriage
   PAGE 20 *"Having gotten . . . to give for [her]."*: DCML, p. 15
   PAGE 20 *"I thought . . . wanted to."*: DCMM, p. 36
   PAGE 21 *"to read . . . of figures."*: TF, p. 52
   PAGE 23 *"It was . . . the heart."*: TRA, p. 24
   PAGE 24 *"as savage . . . meat ax."*: DCHCM, p. 39

Chapter 4: A Scout and Indian Fighter
   PAGE 30 *"The enemy . . . or sit."*: DCML, p. 24
   PAGE 32 *"I . . . had often . . . way at all."*: TRA, p. 26

PAGE 35 *"The first . . . his shoulders."*: DCMM, p. 68

PAGE 36 *"burning . . . kiln."*: DCHCM, p. 48

PAGE 36 *"just . . . soldier."*: DCHCM, p. 49

PAGE 39 *"We all . . . without it."*: TF, p. 76

Chapter 5: A Man of Substance

PAGE 42 *"Death, that . . . loving wife."*: DCML, p. 33

PAGE 43 *"good, industrious . . . comfortable."*: DCHCM, p. 62

PAGE 47 *"I was so . . . with brown paper."*: TF, p. 83

PAGE 49 *"Catch that . . . or alive."*: DCMM, p. 104

PAGE 49 *"dander up . . . to see."*: TF, p. 91

Chapter 6: A Backwoods Politician

PAGE 51 *"I never . . . deceive you."*: DCML, p. 107

PAGE 50-51 *"The thought . . . for a speech."*: DC, p. 82

Chapter 7: Hunter and Bear Killer

PAGE 57 *"There [had] . . . fallen timber."*: DCML, p. 75

PAGE 57 *"There [had] . . . fallen timber."*: DCML, p. 75

PAGE 60 *"I was met . . . my [crop]."*: DCML, p. 56

Chapter 8: Mr. Crockett Goes to Washington

PAGE 64 *"I believe . . . they may."*: DCMM, p. 158

PAGE 64 *"I told . . . at my expense."*: TF, p. 113

PAGE 68 *"met with . . . we all parted."*: DCML, pp. 78-79

PAGE 69 *"I have thought . . . am Recovering."*: TRA, p. 126

PAGE 74 *"He associated himself . . . him an inch."*: TF, pp. 156-157

PAGE 76 *"I believe . . . hypocritically immortalized."* DCMM, p. 158

Chapter 9: Political Disappointments

PAGE 78 *"Since you. . . go to Texas."*: TF, p.225.

PAGE 82 *"As the public . . . being true."*: DCHOS, p. 1

PAGE 82 *"My heart . . . [potato]."*: DCHOS, p. 26

PAGE 83 *"Andrew Jackson . . . into rich."*: TF, p. 206

PAGE 86 *"[They] are as . . . of public money."*: TF, pp. 208-208

Chapter 10: Off to Texas

PAGE 91 *"[I would] rather be . . . United States."*: TRA, p. 414

PAGE 93 *"and [to] give . . . to freedom."*: JLT, p. 18

PAGE 93 *"off to Texas."*: TRA, p. 411

PAGE 93 *"have Santa . . . for a watch seal."*: TRA, p. 411

PAGE 93-94 *"rather be . . . the United States."*: TRA, p. 414

PAGE 98 *"I have . . . high Private,"*: JLT, p. 180

Chapter 11: Remember the Alamo!

PAGE 99 *"I am besieged . . . Santa Anna."*: TRA, p. 541

PAGE 101 *"Sister, do . . . you kindly."*: TRA, p. 544

PAGE 102 *"To the People . . . the World."*: TRA, p. 541

PAGE 102 *"I am besieged . . . or Death."*: TRA, p. 591

PAGE 104 *"You have no . . . for cover."*: JLT, p. 197

Image Credits

© North Wind Picture Archives / Alamy: 8
© CORBIS: 78, 79, 90, 95
© Archivo Iconografico, S.A./CORBIS. 25
© Bettmann/Corbis: 3, 10, 16, 28, 30, 56, 63, 64, 67, 71, 81, 87, 92, 97, 101, 103, 104, 106, 108, 109, 110, 116
© William A. Blake/Corbis: 22
© Gary W. Carter/Corbis: 4
© Richard Cummins/Corbis: 117
© Lowell Georgia/Corbis: 61
© Gunter Marx Photography/Corbis: 66
© Historical Picture Archive/Corbis: 69
© David Muench/Corbis: 58, 94
Lea Phillips/www.flickr.com: 43
Allan Grant/Time Life Pictures/Getty Images: 115
John Giorno Collection: 18
The Granger Collection, New York: 15, 27, 31, 33, 53, 70, 80
© iStockphoto.com/"Phil Cardamone": 26
© iStockphoto.com/"Christopher Badzioch": 46
Library of Congress: 5, 6, 13, 21, 29, 37, 39, 40, 41, 48, 49, 55, 65, 72, 73, 74, 77, 82, 83, 85, 89, 91, 96, 100, 107, 111, 113, 114
Map by Jim McMahon: 2
Mary Evans Picture Library/Mark Furness: 62
© North Wind Picture Archives: 35, 57
Public Broadcasting System: 24
Smithsonian Institution, National Museum of American History: 45
Texas State Library and Archives Commission: 102
Cover art: The Granger Collection, New York

About the Author

George E. Stanley received his doctorate in African linguistics from the University of Port Elizabeth in South Africa. He is now Professor of African and Middle-Eastern Languages and Linguistics at Cameron University in Lawton, Oklahoma, where he teaches Arabic, Persian, Swahili, and Urdu. He is also a well-known children's author, with one hundred books to his credit, including several critically acclaimed biographies.

Index

Discover interesting personalities
in the Sterling Biographies® series: